W9-ARX-101

ELVIS
PRESLEY
Album

PUBLICATIONS INTERNATIONAL, LTD.

Copyright ©1998 Publications International, Ltd. All rights reserved.
This book may not be reproduced or quoted in whole or in part by any
means whatsoever without written permission from:

Louis Weber, C.E.O.
Publications International, Ltd.
7373 North Cicero Avenue
Lincolnwood, Illinois 60646

Permission is never granted for commercial purposes.

Manufactured in U.S.A.

8 7 6 5 4 3 2 1

ISBN: 0-7853-2190-X

4

CONTENTS

1950's
page 6

1960's
page 44

1970's
page 66

New singing sensation
Elvis Presley

Memphis Press-Scimitar, July 28, 1954

IN A SPIN—Elvis Presley can be forgiven for going round and round in more ways than one these days. A 19-year-old Humes High graduate, he has just signed a recording contract with Sun Record Co. of Memphis, and already has a disk out that promises to be the biggest hit that Sun has ever pressed.

It all started when Elvis dropped into Sun's studios one day to cut a personal record at his own expense. Sam Phillips, president of the company, monitored the session and was so impressed with the unusual quality in the young man's voice that he jotted down his name and address. Some time later, Phillips came across a ballad which he thought might be right for Presley's voice. They recorded it; it didn't click. But they tried again; this time with "Blue Moon of Kentucky," a folk standard, backed by "That's All Right Mama."

Just now reaching dealers' shelves, the record is getting an amazing number of plays on all Memphis radio stations. "The odd thing about it," says Marion Keisker of the Sun office, "is that both sides seem to be equally popular on popular, folk and race record programs. This boy has something that seems to appeal to everybody."

"We've just gotten the sample records out to the disk jockeys and distributors in other cities," she said, "but we got big orders yesterday from Dallas and Atlanta." Sun, started by Sam Phillips, former WREC engineer, several years ago, has 40 distributors from coast to coast, so there's a good chance of a big national sale.

Elvis, son of Mr. and Mrs. Vernon Presley, 462 Alabama, is a truck driver for Crown Electric Co. He has been singing and playing the guitar since he was about 13—just, picked it up himself. The home folks who have been hearing him on records so often during the past few weeks can see Elvis in person when he's presented by Disk Jockey Bob Neal in a hillbilly show at Overton Park Shell Friday night along with veteran entertainers from the *Louisiana Hayride.*

Elvis' combo-Bill Black on doghouse bass and Scotty Moore on guitar

Sam Phillips signed Elvis to Sun Records in 1954.

The Commercial Appeal, Memphis, July 25, 1954

SHELL SHOW FRIDAY

Hillbilly Hoedown Features Popular Music Favorites

Favorite folk ballads in a sylvan setting are on the entertainment bill this week as Slim Whitman, one of the top-ranking rural rhythm experts, brings his troupe here for a show at 8 p.m. Friday at the Overton Park Shell.

Whitman is based with the *Louisiana Hayride* group at Shreveport, La., and is currently hitting the top with a variety of rustic records. His left-handed style with the guitar is as unusual as his style of singing.

Also featured will be Billy Walker, a tall Texan, "Sugar-Foot" Collins, "Sonny" Harvelle, Tinker Fry, and "Curly" Harris along for the laughs.

Advance tickets go on sale tomorrow at Walgreen's Main and Union, Bob Neal, WMPS disc jockey and impresario of the Friday show, said yesterday.

Elvis poses in the parking lot of the Eagle's Nest, where he frequently performed.

Memphis Press-Scimitar   October 13, 1954

Hayride Show Signs Elvis Presley

Elvis Presley, Memphis boy who made so good singing and playing the guitar that he has recorded for Sun Record Co. ("Blue Moon of Kentucky" and "That's All Right, Mama"), was a guest on *Louisiana Hayride*. And now he has made even better, Sun announced. He has been signed up for a year's contract with Louisiana Hayride and will be heard in Memphis every third Saturday when CBS picks up the show.

Elvis played the Grand Ole Opry in October.

Elvis became a regular on the Louisiana Hayride that same month.

Memphis Press-Scimitar, October 20, 1954

ELVIS PRESLEY 'CLICKS'

Young Memphis Singer Now In Louisiana Show

Elvis Presley, Memphis' swiftly rising young hillbilly singing star is now a regular member of the *Louisiana Hayride*, broadcast each Saturday night over KWKH, Shreveport, La., and in part each third week over CBS, heard locally over WREC at 8pm.

The *Hayride* specializes in picking promising young rural rhythm talent— and it took just one guest appearance last Saturday for the young Memphian to become a regular. He had been heard about two weeks earlier on *Grand Ole Opry* from Nashville.

Presley was assured by A.M. "Pappy" Covington of the *Hayride* staff that he will be heard over the network portion of the show after he wowed 'em with the songs from his two jukebox hit records made for the Sun Record Co. of Memphis.

In 1954-55, Elvis appeared
with country stars Carl Smith (top left),
Faron Young (top right), and Johnny Cash (bottom).

Memphis Press-Scimitar   AUGUST 6, 1955

AUDIENCE PULLERS . . . . Overton Park Shell was jammed with an overflow audience last night for the wind-up of the eighth annual Bob Neal country music jamboree series.

Several hundred who wanted to hear in person Johnny Cash and Elvis Presley and Webb Pierce and some 22 other country music and comedy performers had to be turned away, while 4000 more lucky people enjoyed the show. The company also toured Little Rock, Ark., 3000 listeners; Camden, Ark., 2000; Sheffield, Ala, 2800; and Tupelo, Miss., 300, this week.

Both Cash and Presley record for Memphis' own Sun Record label.

Memphis Singer Presley Signed By RCA-Victor for Recording Work

By ROBERT JOHNSON *Press-Scimitar Staff*

Elvis Presley, 20, Memphis recording star and entertainer who zoomed into bigtime and the big money almost overnight, has been released from his contract with Sun Record Co. of Memphis and will record exclusively for RCA-Victor, it was announced by Sam C. Phillips, Sun President.

Phillips and RCA officials did not reveal terms, but said the money involved is probably the highest ever paid for a contract release for a country-western recording artist.

"I feel Elvis is one of the most talented youngsters today," Phillips said, "and by releasing his contract to RCA-Victor we will give him the opportunity of entering the largest organization of its kind in the world, so his talents can be given the fullest opportunity."

Handled by Parker

Negotiations were handled by Col. Tom Parker of Hank Snow-Jamboree Attractions, Madison, Tenn., Bob Neal, Presley's personal manager, and Coleman Tiley III of RCA-Victor.

Elvis Presley Music, a publishing firm, has been set up to handle much of Presley's music, in conjunction with Hill and Range Music, Inc., New York City.

Bob Neal, WMPS personality, continues as Presley's personal manager and will handle his personal appearances and other activities, but Hank Snow-Jamboree Attractions will handle Presley enterprises in radio, TV, movies and theaters.

Also taking part in negotiations were Hank Snow himself, RCA-Victor's longest-term western star; Sam Eagre, RCA-Victor regional sales manager; Ben Starr of Hill and Range music, and Jim Crudington, local RCA-Victor representative.

Presley, who lived in Tupelo, Miss., until he was 14 and is a graduate of Humes High.

Phillips signed him for Sun Records after Presley wandered in one day and wanted to have a recording made at his own expense.

Cashbox, trade journals, named him the most promising western star. He became a regular on *Louisiana Hayride* on CBS. His newest record, "Mystery Train" and "I Forgot to Remember," is his best-seller so far. Both songs were written by Stan Kesler and Charlie Feathers, a Memphis team. Tony Arden has just recorded "I Forgot to Remember" for Victor, and Peewee King's latest is also a Kesler-Feathers composition. All five Presley records have made the best-seller list.

Presley's "Mystery Train" is now being played by pop disk jockeys as well as c&w in the east.

Sun has 10 country-western artists remaining on its label, including Johnny Cash and a newcomer, Carl Perkins of Bermis, Tenn., who writes his own music and is causing a stir. This week Sun brings out a new feminine vocalist, Maggie Sun Wimberly of Florence, Ala., with songs by another Memphis composing team, Bill Cantrell and Quentin Church, who wrote a previous substantial country-western hit, "Day Dreaming."

Elvis records his first album for RCA in January 1956.

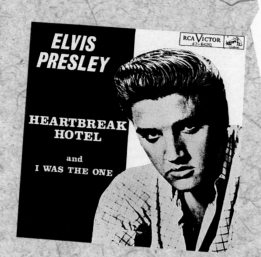

ELVIS PRESLEY

Heartbreak Hotel (Tree, BMI)
I Was the One (Jungnickel, ASCAP)—Victor
6420—Presley's first Victor disk might easily break
in both markets. "Heartbreak Hotel" is a strong
blues item wrapped up in his usual powerful style
and a great beat. "I Was the One" is about as close to
r&b as you can get without horns, and has more pop
appeal. Presley is riding high right now with network
TV appearances, and the disc should benefit from
all the special plugging.

After Elvis signed with RCA, he evolved from
a local country performer into a nationally
known rock 'n' roller.

The Boundless Future
MOVIES SIGN ELVIS

Hal Wallis, motion-picture producer in Hollywood, heard the screams of the teen-agers as clearly as if he'd been accompanying Elvis Presley on his sensational cross-country tour. They sounded louder in his ear as he sat in a crowded night-club room in Las Vegas—sounded louder than the sophisticated sneers of the well-groomed audience who came to stare at Elvis. Quietly, Hal Wallis made his way backstage after the show and without fanfare, held out the promise of a screen test for Elvis, the screen test that this boy has longed for ever since he dreamed the big dreams of long ago. Skeptics in Hollywood laughed. But Wallis sensed an ability in Elvis far and above that exhibited by his singing and his guitar playing.

To quote the Western Editor of *PHOTOPLAY* magazine: "I went to look at the screen test that Presley made, with considerable doubt in my mind about this boy's acting ability," Norman Siegal wrote. "But, when he went into his scene with veteran Frank Faylen, I got excited. This boy is an actor." Norman Siegal was seeing in this test what Hal Wallis instinctively knew was there. Hal is having a screenplay written especially for Elvis and his name will soon be on every movie marquee in the country. Watch for it and see for yourself whether *PHOTOPLAY* and Hal Wallis are any judges of talent.

Producer Hal Wallis (far left) signed Elvis to a movie deal.

Elvis and his combo failed to shake up Vegas.

Variety   May 2, 1956

New Frontier, Las Vegas

Las Vegas, April 25
Freddy Martin Orch (17) with Martin Men (5), Johnny Cochrane, Dave Leonard, Bob Hunter, Shecky Green, Elvis Presley & Combo (3), Venus Starlets (14), Jack Teigen, Marge Baker; $2 minimum. . .

. . . Elvis Presley, coming in on a wing of advance hoopla, doesn't hit the mark here in a spot surfeited with rock and rollers playing in shifts in every cocktail lounge all over the Strip. The loud braying of the tunes which rocketed him to the bigtime is wearing, and the applause comes back edged with a polite sound . . . .

Memphis Press-Scimitar   January 11, 1956

Memphis Boy, Elvis Presley, Signs Contract With Gleason

By ROBERT JOHNSON, Press-Scimitar Staff Writer

One more giant step toward the biggest time by Elvis Presley, the 20-year-old former Humes High boy whose career has zoomed in little more than a year.

Elvis, whose recording contract with Sun Records was recently acquired by RCA-Victor, has been contracted for four appearances by Jackie Gleason on the half-hour *Stage Show* which Gleason produces along with his own show on Saturday nights.

The first appearance on the CBS show, which we get through WREC-TV, will be Jan. 28, with others on Feb. 4, 11, and 18.

NBC also was reported as having been bidding for Elvis. They wanted him for *The Perry Como Show*, opposite Gleason.

Events are spinning faster than his records for the Memphis youngster whose songs have appealed to fans of three musical categories— country and western, rock 'n' roll and straight pop. Don't let your head spin with them Elvis!

Elvis rocks out on Stage Show.

Scotty Moore's guitar provided the driving rhythm to Elvis' rock 'n' roll sound.

Eventually, Elvis appeared on Stage Show 6 times.

13

Time   June 18, 1956

Yeh-Heh-Heh-Hes, Baby

In Boston, Roman Catholic leaders urged that the offensive music be boycotted. In Hartford city officials considered revoking the State Theater's license after several audiences got too rowdy during a musical stage show. In Washington the police chief recommended banning such shows from the National Guard Armory after brawls in which several people were injured . . .

. . . The object of all this attention is a musical style known as "rock 'n' roll," which has captivated U.S. adolescents as swing captivated prewar teen-agers and ragtime vibrated those of the '20s . . .

. . . There is no denying that rock 'n' roll evokes a physical response from even its most reluctant listeners, for that giant pulse matches the rhythmical operations of the human body, and the performers are all too willing to specify it. Said an Oakland, California policeman, after watching Elvis ("The Pelvis") Presley . . . last week: "If he did that in the street, we'd arrest him . . . ."

Elvis was labeled dangerous by adults.

The press and mainstream public attacked Elvis for his performing style, music, hair, clothing, and accent.

Newsweek   May 14, 1956

Music:
Hillbilly on a Pedestal

The high-pitched squeals of females in fanatic teen-age packs are being heard again. Elvis Presley, a hillbilly singer capable of impressive bodily contortions has moved onto the pedestal lately occupied by Johnnie Ray and, before him, by Frank Sinatra . . . .

Last week Presley wound up his first night-club date, a two-week stand at the New Frontier Hotel in Las Vegas. Wedged into a show built around Freddy Martin's silken arrangements of Tchaikovsky and show tunes, Elvis was somewhat like a jug of corn liquor at a champagne party. He hollered songs like "Blue Suede Shoes" and "Heartbreak Hotel," and his bodily motions were embarrassingly specific . . . .

AFTER LAST NIGHT

Squeals Drown Presley's Songs

Elvis Presley, young bump and grind artist, turned a rainy Sunday afternoon into an orgy of squealing in St. Paul auditorium.

He vibrated his hips so much, and the 3,000 customers squealed so insistently at the vibrations, it was impossible to hear him sing. None of the smitten seemed to care . . . .

. . . A radio interviewer asked him about his record successes.

'I switched to Victor because that's the biggest company there is,' drawled Presley. 'You 19 or 21?' asked another. 'I've heard both.' 'Twenty-one,' answered Presley. 'Wish ah was 19.' Presley came here from Memphis, Tennessee, his home. He's been so busy he hasn't had a chance to get home for awhile. He got a few free days by surprise after he flopped at a Las Vegas, Nevada, night club. They replaced him with a girl singer. The older customers in Las Vegas just didn't dig him . . . .

Elvis' unique style of dress drove the press crazy.

Elvis' effect on his female fans was quite controversial.

America   June 23, 1956

Beware Elvis Presley

Does the name Elvis Presley mean anything to you? If it doesn't the chances are that it does to your children. He is a "singer" of rock 'n' roll songs and his records are top favorites with the juke-box audience. If his "entertainment" could be confined to records, it might not be too bad an influence on the young, but unfortunately Presley makes personal appearances . . .

. . . Yet the National Broadcasting Company wasn't loathe to bring Presley into the living-rooms of the nation on the evening of June 5. Appearing on *The Milton Berle Show*, Presley fortunately, didn't go so far as he did in LaCrosse, but his routine was "in appalling taste" (said the San Francisco *Chronicle*) . . . .

The controversy surrounding Elvis ignited after his performance on The Milton Berle Show.

It was this provocative version of "Hound Dog" on Berle's show that created the uproar.

A Tux for TV

A bubblegum card
of the Allen show

Elvis in a comedy sketch
with Steve Allen and
Imogene Coca

Newsweek   July 16, 1956

Lardner's Week

Devitalizing Elvis

by John Lardner

... Live and let live—that is how most of us boys in the upper crust of sociology look at it. Nonetheless, we all watched with interest last week when one of our number, Steve Allen (who has his own show, as we say in the scientific game), made a public attempt to neutralize, calm, or de-twitch Elvis Presley, the lively singer ....

... Allen's ethics were questionable from the start. He fouled Presley, a fair-minded judge would say, by dressing him like a corpse, in white tie and tails. This is a costume often seen on star performers at funerals, but only when the deceased has specifically requested it in his will. Elvis had made no such request—or, for that matter, no will. He was framed ....

Time   July 23, 1956

Sunday at 8

When NBC's Steve Allen decisively beat CBS's Ed Sullivan a fortnight ago in the battle for TV's Sunday-at-8 audience ..., the burning question among television's hucksters was: Who had done it, Allen or his guest star Elvis ("The Pelvis") Presley? Sullivan, in the unaccustomed position of runner-up, affected disdain for the Pelvis, snorted that he would not have the gyrating groaner at any price on his family-type program. "He is not my cup of tea," Sullivan said loftily ....

Elvis appears
in a tuxedo for his
appearance on
The Steve Allen Show.

Allen used comedy to
soften Elvis' image
as a notorious
rock 'n' roller, a
tactic that defused
the controversy.

Jacksonville, Florida, August 11, 1956

Elvis' Performance Satisfies Gooding

Elvis Presley, minus his bump and grind dance, continued his two-day show in Jacksonville today after a hectic time yesterday—a warning from a judge and trouble with the Variety Artist Guild.

The teen-age rock 'n' roll idol, who was advised before his first show here yesterday to 'keep it clean' or face court charges, met with local Juvenile Court Judge Marion Gooding after the opening performance and was warned sternly to remove the objectionable hip movements from the act.

Judge Gooding, who watched the first performance along with 2,200 screaming youngsters, said today apparently Presley has complied with the order, judging from reports of the later shows last night.

Before talking to Gooding yesterday, Presley appeared bewildered at the request. 'I can't figure out what I'm doing wrong,' he told reporters backstage.

'I know my mother approves of what I'm doing . . . If I had a teen-age sister, I certainly would not object to her coming to watch a show like this,' he said.

Meanwhile, a representative of the American Guild of Variety Artists told Presley yesterday that unless he joined AGVA and his manager, Tom Parker, posted bond and insurance for other acts in the Presley show, AGVA would prevent other acts from appearing.

The matter was cleared up shortly before show time when Presley accepted membership in the organization and his manager accepted bond and insurance obligations to AGVA.

Presley, who kept a nonchalant attitude throughout the day, spent his spare time between performances posing for magazine, television and newspaper photographers and answering reporters' questions.

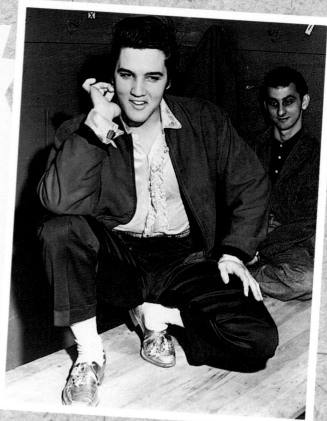

ELVIS: " I just act the way I feel."

Elvis tones down his act in Jacksonville.

LOOK   August 7, 1956

. . . Presley is mostly nightmare. On-stage, his gyrations, his nose wiping, his leers are vulgar. When asked about the sex element in his act, he answers without blinking his big brown eyes: "Ah don't see anything wrong with it. Ah just act the way Ah feel." But Elvis will also grin and say, "Without mah left leg, Ah'd be dead." Old friends, like the Memphis Press-Scimitar's Bob Johnson, advise him to clean up his "dances."

Presley has taken the rock 'n' roll craze to new sales heights. He has also dragged "big beat" music to new lows in taste.

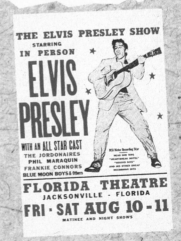

THE ELVIS PRESLEY SHOW
STARRING
IN PERSON
ELVIS PRESLEY
WITH AN ALL STAR CAST
THE JORDONAIRES
PHIL MARAQUIN
FRANKIE CONNORS
BLUE MOON BOYS & others
FLORIDA THEATRE
JACKSONVILLE - FLORIDA
FRI · SAT AUG 10 - 11
MATINEE AND NIGHT SHOWS

LETTERS To The Editors

ELVIS

Sirs:
I'm an Elvis Presley fan writing you to thank you for the nine-page article on him ("Elvis—a Different Kind of Idol." Life, August 27). Some time ago you had a short article on him. That was good but I really flipped when I saw this story.
JUDY MCCLELLAND
White Plains, N.Y.

Sirs:
We want to thank you for that picture spread you had about our "dream baby"—Elvis. It was the "badest," and when I say the "badest," that means the "greatest." The "cats" here in Philly are wild about Elvis. He's the "king," the supreme ruler.
STELLA VERBIT
Philadelphia, Pa.

Sirs:
Please don't give people the wrong impressions of Elvis Presley. We think he's the absolute end.
JANIS OLSEN
Grand Junction, Colo.

Sirs:
No one complains about the female strip-teasers but when it comes to Elvis, it's a different story. When he was on the Milton Berle show the criticisms started flying. But when a girl danced the way an uncivilized native would, no one said a thing. That really scorched me.
CAROL PARKER
Rochester, N.Y.

Sirs:
Few stories featuring Elvis Presley seem to include much about his family or his parents. Could you tell me if he has any brothers or sisters?
BOBBIE JEAN POLEET
Hanover, Ind.

No sisters; a twin brother died at birth.—ED.

The antics of Elvis' devoted fans caused parents and teachers to worry.

Breaking hearts with just a glance!

Presley's 82.6% Share
Ed Sullivan show hit an all-time peak in share of audience Sunday night (9), swamping NBC-TV's feature film showing of "The Magic Box" with an 82.6% share, compared with NBC's 8.3% . . . .

Elvis appeared on <u>The Ed Sullivan Show</u> three times. For his third appearance, Sullivan ordered that Elvis be shown on camera only from the waist up.

Tupelo, Miss., Fair, With Elvis, Sets Gate, Grandstand Records

Tupelo, Miss.—Elvis Presley and the Mississippi-Alabama Fair & Dairy Show rocked and rolled to smashing success.

The six-day fair, which closed Saturday (29), piled up an all-time record attendance of 180,000. Grandstand receipts were 40 percent higher than last year, and the midway gross (by the Olson Shows) topped that for 1955 by 12 per cent.

Presley, in for his home-coming (he was born in East Tupelo), wowed 'em on his day, Wednesday (26). No fewer than 100 special police, including 50 State highway patrolman, were called in to control the crowd that stormed the grandstand to see the Tupelo boy made good.

His End $11,000

Mississippi's Gov. J. P. Coleman was on hand to present a scroll to Presley and say the State was proud of Tupelo's native son. Mayor James Vallard joined in like expressions.

Presley received $11,800 for his appearance, with his end based on 60 per cent of grandstand receipts. He was in on a guarantee of $5,000 against the percentage. For his appearance the usual grandstand price was upped from 75 cents to $1.50. The capacity, moreover, had been increased by the addition of 3,000 seats in front of the stage.

Bill Changed Daily

The rock and roll headliner provided the highlight of the fair, but actually was part of the sweeping changes effected by the fair's manager, J. M. Savery. Each day, for the first time, the fair offered name or semi-name talent in front of the grandstand at 75 cents admission.

Ernest Tubb and His Texas Troubadours, the Wilburn Brothers, Hank Locklin and Bobb Helms were in opening day, The Blackwood Brothers and the Statesmen were offered Thursday (27). Wally Fowler and His Chuck Wagon Gang, the Bond Sisters, Oak Ridge Quartet and Sister Kate Freeman were in Friday (28), and Carl Perkins, Johnny Mack Brown, Smiley Burnette, Warren (rock and roll Ruby) Smith and Eddy Bond and the Stompers the final day, all on a two-a-day basis.

In prior years the fair offered the same show for the duration of its run.

Savery, commenting on the success this year, said that the fair will continue to offer different attractions each day next year.

22G for Attractions

The grandstand attraction outlay was $22,000, an all-time high here but more than warranted, Savery said. The fair's attendance surpassed the old mark by 24,000, but receipts from all sources were proportionately higher than the jump in attendance.

Besides the shift in attractions, the fair made many other changes. A new stage was built, new cattle and swine barns were erected, premiums were hiked to $20,000 and there were more industrial exhibits because space was freed by reducing the independent midway. An automobile was given away nightly. All available exhibit space was sold out, and livestock entries hit a new high.

Elvis performs at the Miss.-Ala. Fair and Dairy Show in his hometown of Tupelo.

23

DIG

january 1957 25¢

FOR TEENAGERS ONLY

• GENE VINCENT

• COOL HOT ROD

• SO YOU WANT TO BE A MODEL?

INTERNATIONAL PEN PALS

SCENES FROM PRESLEY'S FIRST MOVIE!

WHO'S COOL?
The Cat That Wears Levi's, Peggers or Ivy League?

The many faces of Elvis Presley: A sentimental publicity photo to soften his image (top left); an introspective moment at home (top right); the sullen face of a rebel idol (bottom).

24

HEARTBREAK: HOUND DOGS PUT SALES ZIP INTO PRESLEY PRODUCTS

Firms turn out Elvis-labeled shoes, jeans, lipstick but fear fate of Davy Crockett.

NEWSWEEK

ENTERPRISE:

Presley Spells Profit

. . . "It's nothing new," [Hank] Saperstein explains. "It happened with Valentino, Theda Bara, and Clara Bow. We are each of us insecure in our way. We like to identify ourselves with people who are somebody." Identifying himself with Presley seemed the thing for Saperstein to do; already handling products with the imprimaturs of Wyatt Earp, the Lone Ranger, and Lassie, Saperstein signed up Elvis for an exclusive merchandising deal, pledging to do for Presley at the retail counter what Col. Tom Parker did for him on stage, screen, TV, and records.

Presley Products: Teen-agers have since mobbed the retail counters in search of Presley products. Dollar lipsticks (in exotic shades of Hound Dog Orange and Tutti Frutti Red) have passed the 450,000 mark in sales. A Providence, R.I., costume-jewelry firm has turned out 350,000 charm bracelets ($1 plus tax), jangling with such Presley symbols as a hound dog, guitar, or a cracked heart. Another $150,000 has gone for the same number of statuettes of Elvis, complete with guitar. A New York clothing manufacturer has moved 80,000 pairs of $2.98 jeans bearing Presley's photo and has expanded the line to include Presley "Ivy League" girls' shirts. ("Ivy League" pants are next . . . .)

Sensational
YOUR OWN GENUINE, OFFICIAL

Elvis Presley

DOLL

ONLY DOLL OF ITS KIND APPROVED BY ELVIS PRESLEY

The thrill of your lifetime! Now *you* can have "Elvis Presley" for YOURSELF! He'll be your companion—morning, noon, and *night time, too!* Naturally, we can't bring you the real, live singing sensation, but we can give you the NEXT best thing—a real wonderful Doll that looks just like Elvis, stands like Elvis, gyrates like Elvis, in fact, does everything except sing like Elvis! You'll *love* this genuine Elvis Presley Doll.

Wait until you see him! You'll swoon with excitement. It looks SO real! From Elvis's blue suede shoes, to blue jeans, open-collared plaid shirt, long, wavy molded hair, sideburns, and handsome looks, you'll scream, "That *IS* Elvis!"

This Elvis Doll, the one and only GENUINE, OFFICIAL Elvis Presley Doll, is a big one-foot and one-half tall! And perfectly proportioned, just like the world-famous star of Records, Movies, TV, Radio, Stage, etc. etc.

When your friends see your Elvis Presley doll they'll want to tear it out of your hands, so be prepared! Hang on tight! But, first BE SURE you GET your Elvis Doll. So order NOW before our limited supply is gone! We reserve the right to return your money when our supply of Elvis Presley Dolls is gone. So HURRY! Send money — $3.98 plus 27¢ postage and packing — or $4.25 in all. Or order C.O.D. and pay your mailman. But, for your sake, PLEASE hurry! Send your order TODAY! Satisfaction absolutely guaranteed or your money cheerfully refunded.

ELVIS PRESLEY DOLL HEADQUARTERS
Dept. 112 228 Lexington Ave., New York, N. Y.

only $3.98

Love Me Tender

RUSH THIS COUPON!

ELVIS PRESLEY DOLL HEADQUARTERS,
Dept. 112
228 Lexington Ave., New York, N. Y.
Please send me _____ Elvis Presley Dolls, Send prepaid—$3.98 plus 27¢ postage and packing, or $4.25 in all.
Send me _____ Elvis Dolls C.O.D.
BE SURE to rush my order!

My name _____
Address _____

MONEY BACK GUARANTEE!

60 — HEP CAT'S

When Elvis signed a deal with merchandiser Hank Saperstein, teens mobbed stores looking for Presley products.

Is he a new JAMES DEAN?

When Elvis got into close-up love scenes with Debra Paget "the camera boys hung their eyes out a foot." "What technique!" one of them said later.

And Debra said: "That Elvis Presley! He doesn't need any stand-ins!"—a crack at some of the matinee idols who reach Hollywood via a boast about their ability to slay the lady stars.

"Oh brother!" said movie director Robert Webb when they told him he had to handle the rock 'n' roll phenomenon.

"Oh Elvis? He's a nice, co-operative guy," Webb was soon saying.

Studio chief Hal Wallis has let it leak that he considers Presley the natural successor to his discovery of four years ago, the late James Dean.

Critics who have seen the film rushes say Presley sometimes looks as if he could emulate Dean in the intensity of his screen work. But they wonder if he's not the "singing Marlon Brando."

The three songs in the film, in addition to the title tune, are "Poor Boy," "You're Gonna Move," and "Let Me." The discs will be out shortly in advance of the film due here in December.

Presley has been good enough actor for the studios to bring forward the date of his second picture, *Lonesome Cowboy*, in which he stars with bare-all Jayne Mansfield . . . .

Many in Hollywood wondered if Elvis Presley would become the new James Dean.

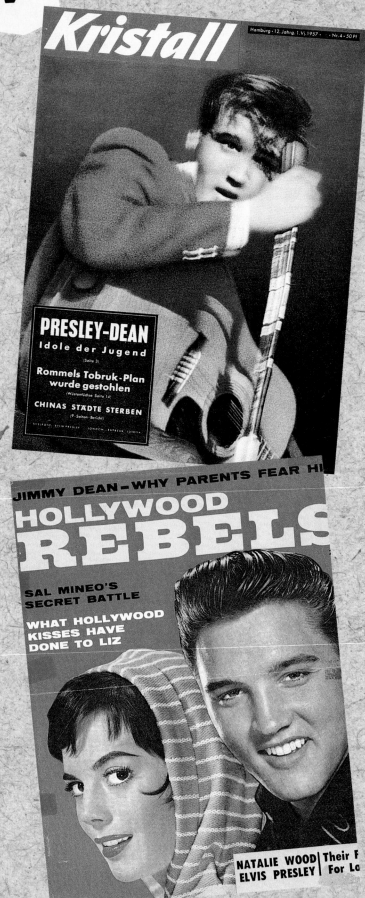

Kristall

Hamburg · 12. Jahrg. 1. Vj. 1957 · Nr. 4 · 50 Pf

PRESLEY-DEAN
Idole der Jugend
(Seite 3)

Rommels Tobruk-Plan wurde gestohlen
(Wüstenfüchse Seite 14)

CHINAS STÄDTE STERBEN
(9-Seiten-Bericht)

TITELFOTO: ELVIS PRESLEY · LONDON-EXPRESS · LUTETIA

JIMMY DEAN – WHY PARENTS FEAR HI

HOLLYWOOD REBELS

SAL MINEO'S SECRET BATTLE

WHAT HOLLYWOOD KISSES HAVE DONE TO LIZ

NATALIE WOOD | Their F
ELVIS PRESLEY | For Lo

Elvis dated Dean's costar Natalie Wood (top) and was photographed with Dean pals Sal Mineo (bottom left) and Nick Adams (bottom right).

ELVIS PRESLEY
Becomes a Movie Star

They were all set to jeer. They remained to cheer him instead...

As far as the people of Hollywood knew, Elvis Presley was merely the most sensational, controversial, personality to hit the town in a coon's age. Now they know different—at least the lucky few who really got close to Elvis. Listen to his co-players in *Love Me Tender*. Bill Campbell: "When you see a guy this sweet, who wants to work as hard, you have to like him. He's a smart boy and a good boy." Richard Egan: "He broke me up when we got in a scene together. He'd look me right in the eye and throw me. The right thing just seems to come naturally to him. I think he has an unlimited future, and I think he can do anything he attempts." Debra Paget: "He's amazing. He's so unspoiled and fresh, everybody is crazy about him. In fact, he's more fun than a barrel of monkeys! And he is a gentleman."

Elvis looks as though he enjoyed working on his first movie, Love Me Tender.

28

Even Elvis' youngest fans couldn't wait to see him on the big screen.

LOVE ME TENDER
Elvis Presley's first

Elvis is here, and to say anything else is probably superfluous. But he's here, and of course he sings—four songs. And his guitar is here. Elvis has been home on the farm these several years while his big brothers (Richard Egan, William Campbell, James Drury) have been fighting for the South. On their last fight they divested some Union soldiers of 12,000 dollars cash. Unknown to them, the war was over. The brothers and their buddies—Neville Brand among them—sit down and decide to split the loot since the General they were going to deliver it to doesn't have an army to spend it on. Richard Egan can use the money because also home on the farm are his mother (Mildred Dunnock) and his intended (Debra Paget). Unknown to Egan they think he has been killed in the war and Debra has married Elvis. "Love Me Tender," Elvis sings on the front porch the first night the family is all together, and Richard can hardly stand it. He decides he must go away or his love for Debra will eat at him. But there's the money which the Union has come to claim. Hand it over, the U.S. Marshal (Russ Conway) tells Egan, and we'll drop all charges. He's willing to hand it over, so are his brothers, but their buddies—mainly Neville Brand—refuse. It's while Debra is helping Richard collect the money that Neville turns Elvis against them. Elvis becomes insanely jealous. He nearly shakes Debra to death and shoots, but does not kill, the brother he always loved. Then he comes to see that he was wrong. His acting—in this, his first picture—is as good as anyone else's. CinemaScope—20th-Fox.

Memphis Press-Scimitar   December 3, 1956

TV News and Views

By ROBERT JOHNSON   Press-Scimitar Staff Writer

Elvis in Memphis with parents Vernon and Gladys

I never had a better time than yesterday afternoon when I dropped in at Sam Phillips' Sun Record bedlam on Union at Marshall. It was what you might call a barrel-house of fun. Carl Perkins was in a recording session . . . and he has one that's going to hit as hard as "Blue Suede Shoes." We're trying to arrange an advance audition for you Memphis fans before the song is released in January. Johnny Cash dropped in. Jerry Lee Lewis was there, too, and then Elvis stopped by.

Elvis headed for the piano and started to Fats Domino it on "Blueberry Hill." The joint was really rocking before they got thru.

Elvis is high on Jerry Lee Lewis. "That boy can go," he said. "I think he has a great future ahead of him. He has a different style, and the way he plays a piano just gets inside me."

Elvis debunked the newest rumor: "No, I haven't bought 200 acres at Collierville," he said. "How do those stories get started?"

He talked earnestly about the Toledo incident. "I talked to that fellow for at least 15 minutes, trying to be nice to him and keep him from starting anything, but finally it just got out of hand."

I never saw the boy more likeable than [when] he was just fooling around with these other fellows who have the same interest he does.

If Sam Phillips had been on his toes, he'd have turned the recorder on when that very unrehearsed but talented bunch got to cutting up on "Blueberry Hill" and a lot of other songs. That quartet could sell a million.

Despite his fame, Elvis declined to move from his hometown of Memphis. Here, girlfriend Anita Wood welcomes him home.

Top: Elvis shows off his new home, Graceland, to starlet Yvonne Lime.
Right: Elvis blows off some steam while out on the town.

'Loving You' Draws Happy Shrieks From Elvis Presley's Fans

Audience shrieks to Elvis Presley's wriggles are available (for them as likes 'em) again in the Paramount Theater where Mr. Presley wriggles in Vistavision and Technicolor and the tale of an orphan boy's zoom to fame entitled *Loving You*.

Although Mr. Presley's art has improved to the extent that he can generate more shrieks out of much less wriggly wriggles the total shrieks are fewer than during his recent film, *Love Me Tender*, due to the increased amount of plot and high emotions in *Loving You*.

In *Loving You*, a truck-driver, Presley, is discovered by Lizabeth Scott, the very tricky press agent for a lame band, conducted by her divorced husband, Wendell Corey.

The Presley voice, charm and wriggle buoy up the band magnificently but complicated questions arise: Does Mr. Presley love Lizabeth and maybe she him or does he love Dolores Hart, more his age.

* * *

ANYWAY Mr. Corey loves Lizabeth though doubting her motives, and he is fond of Mr. Presley whom he describes as just the type of upstanding and shriek-inducing youth he would love to have for a son. As for Dolores her eyes brim with tears when Presley sings, an odd effect.

Despite all the adulation he inspires, Mr. P. feels friendless and is inclined to question that his rosy road to fame is wholly honorable or the perfect answer to his dreams.

He is saddened by evidence of self-interest on the part of Liz and the tendency of some of the most foolish adults ever seen on any screen to consider him a menace to youth and culture.

When these doddering middle-agers are persuaded by the director to respond to the Presley art with joyous semi-wriggles, you really have something.

All this, one senses, is rather a bore to the shriekers who are happier just shrieking to Presley songs, Hot Dog, Lonesome Cowboy, Let Me Be Your Teddy Bear and Mean Woman Blues.

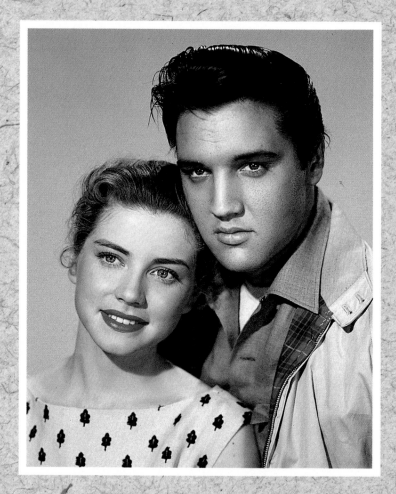

Hal Wallis (bottom) discovered both Elvis and Dolores Hart (top).

Memphis Press-Scimitar   July 10, 1957

Elvis Film Sets Record In Crowds at Strand

And First Day of 'Loving You' Also Breaks All Cash Records Except One

The first day of *Loving You* broke every existing attendance record in the history of the Strand. It also broke every money record except one. The first Saturday run of *The 10 Commandments* brought in $200 more. Its tickets were priced at $2 top, however, against 90 cent top for *Loving You*.

The Presley picture yesterday also almost broke the one-day gross record for Paramount Pictures releases playing at any Memphis theater. Only *The Greatest Show on Earth,* playing at the Malco, with higher prices and twice as many seats, and one other Paramount picture ever took in more money in Memphis in a single day.

Hal Wallis, producer of the picture, telephoned Manager Alex Thompson three times yesterday from Hollywood. The first time to inquire about attendance, the second time to see if the phenomenal business was holding up (it was increasing), and the third time to ask that clippings of reviews and news stories on the picture be air-mailed to him.

Lloyd Bailey, theater manager said, "We've had some good movies here, but I've never seen anything like this."

Today, Presley followers were still flocking to see their idol in "unexpected numbers," according to Bailey. And there has been no letup of lung exercise. Bailey said today's customers were "as loud as yesterday's." He added: "They finally finished ripping off all my billboard displays," including, he said a cardboard cutout of Elvis "which gave them a little trouble at first."

Yesterday, most of the theater's 1100 seats emptied after each performance and were refilled in 15 minutes. Some dyed-in-the-wool Presley fans stayed for as many as five performances, however.

Elvis cuts loose in a scene from Loving You.

Elvis' costars included character actor Wendell Corey, ingenue Hart, and star Lizabeth Scott.

KING ELVIS

ON THE "JAILHOUSE ROCK" MOVIE SET

King Elvis stars in M-G-M's dramatic new story with music, an Avon Production directed by Richard Thorpe and produced by Pandro S. Berman. Co-starring is the late Judy Tyler, with Mickey Shaughnessy, Dean Jones and Jennifer Holden. Guy Trosper wrote the terrific screen play . . . and it turns out to be Elvis Presley's greatest picture. King Elvis sings six hit songs that will meet with your approval.

During the filming of this great M-G-M production . . . the candid photographs on this and the next two following pages were taken for your Hep Cats magazine.

Some of the publicity stills for Jailhouse Rock featured Elvis with a wallaby!

MGM PRÉSENTE UNE PRODUCTION AVON   EN CINEMASCOPE
ELVIS PRESLEY
LE ROCK DU BAGNE
AVEC JUDY TYLER   "JAILHOUSE ROCK"   Réalisateur RICHARD THORPE   Producteur PANDRO S. BERMAN
GEVANGENIS ROCK

In France, the film was called Le Rock du Bagne.

For millions of teenagers this will be counted as The Crime Of The Century. Wars may come and peace may go ... but his fans believed that Elvis Presley's sideburns and mane were here to stay. But how wrong were the fans! As these pictures prove conclusively. For the sake of his rock 'n' rolling art (and a substantial salary), Presley's locks have been shorn for M-G-M's Jailhouse Rock.

The film? A dramatic story set to music. And there's plenty of drama in the expressions on Presley's face as the hair falls from his head. At first: laughing-devil-may-care. Then: realization sinks in. Last: MISERY. Scene of the crime was M-G-M Studios. And the name of the demon barber, the villain of the piece: actor Jack Lorenz. **BURT RAINER**

Publicity maintained that Elvis' hair was cut for <u>Jailhouse Rock</u>, but it was really a wig!

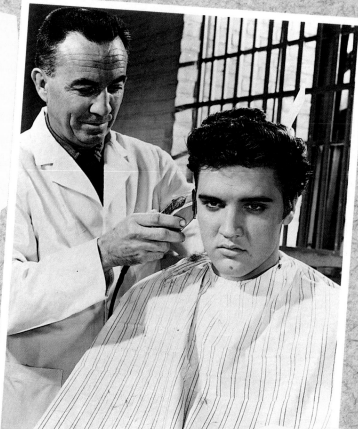

Elvis' costar, Judy Tyler, was killed in an auto accident shortly after filming was completed.

"Jailhouse Rock"

(MGM)   CinemaScope   96 Min.

Cast: Elvis Presley, Judy Tyler, Mickey Shaughnessy, Vaughan Taylor, Jennifer Holden, Dean Jones, Anne Neyland.

Credits: An Avon Prod.; Produced by Pandro S. Berman; Directed by Richard Thorpe; Screenplay by Guy Trosper; Based on a story by Ned Young.

Elvis Presley fans should have a field day with this musical melodrama showcasing their boy. The CinemaScope camera seldom leaves his ever-movin' person as he romps through six songs, becomes involved with three girls, throws several punches, has his sideburns and long hair shorn, displays his bare chest, gets tangled up in a big dance production number and performs countless other acts that have endeared him to his followers in the past. The barely discernible story-line traces the fall and rise of Presley from his jailhouse days to Hollywood.

Serving a prison stretch for an accidental murder, Elvis takes up singing and shortly after his release is on his way to stardom, on records, radio, TV, in clubs and finally in the movies. Embittered, heartless, mercenary, short-tempered, yet somehow sympathetic, Presley is reformed at the end and wins his loyal lady. To be sure, there are a few others in the cast, notably the late Judy Tyler, as his business partner who loses her head over the heel, and Mickey Shaughnessy as a cynical convict. Given some particularly colloquial dialogue, Presley seems to be right at home in the part. Teenagers who like their Elvis all shook up will find much to cheer about here, and the picture should gross accordingly.

Hysterical Shrieks Greet Elvis In His Gold Jacket and Shoes

The trouble with going to see Elvis Presley is that you're liable to get killed. The experience is the closest thing to getting bashed on the head with an atomic bomb.

Elvis gave two performances Sunday in the Olympia—each to shrieking audiences of around 14,000. Presley, the singing troubadour with the long sideburns, gives off more electricity than the Detroit Edison Co.'s combined transmitters.

When he made his grand entrance, pandemonium broke loose and carnage waited in the wings. Most of the afternoon throng were little girls, nice little girls who just adore Elvis. They wore Elvis buttons, Elvis hats and carried Elvis pictures.

Before the show, Elvis sat still long enough for a brief press conference. He didn't seem a bit self-conscious in his red suede jacket, flashy blue shirt and blue pants. Elvis is very polite. "Yes, ma'am" and "yes sir" he was careful to say.

He was asked whether he worried about his popularity waning. "If they forgot me, I'll just have to do something worth remembering," he said. **And what about the Army, Elvis?**

"When I took my physical, they told me it might be three months, six months or a year."

Eight cars are a lot, aren't they, Elvis? Ever thought of selling any of them?

"If I wanted to sell them I wouldn't have bought them in the first place. I just built a new four-car garage. Guess I'll have to build another one for the other four cars."

Elvis came here in a Cadillac limousine from Ft. Wayne, Ind. His young fans were up early trying, to no avail, to track him down.

The young'uns started to congregate at the Olympia as early as 9 p.m. for the 2 o'clock show. Some tried the hotels with no luck.

Inside the Olympia, the youngsters surged against police lines in hope of getting an early look at their idol. "Insane, isn't it?" said one of the 175 policemen assigned to the "Sideburn Detail."

Except for climbing up each other's backs, the crowd was fairly orderly.

The 22-year-old Presley, who had changed into a gold jacket, gold shoes and a gold string tie, dashed on stage to the hysterical shrieks of unleashed bedlam.

Hundred of flashbulbs popped and swoons reached a crescendo, "Elvis, Elvis, Elvis, Elvis."

Before the show, Tom Parker, general manager of the Hillbilly singer, talked about Elvis' popularity.

"We get 25,000 to 30,000 fan letters a week," Parker said. "Why, he even got more than 270,000 Christmas cards, a lot of them from right here in Detroit."

Elvis is a nice boy, said Parker. "None of this has gone to his head."

There is a fanatical loyalty among Presley fans.

A teen-aged girl, sporting a "I Hate Elvis" button, was forced to remove it by a group of fans before they would allow her to reach her seat.

From here Presley will go to Buffalo, thence to Toronto, Ottawa and Philadelphia. Then Elvis will hike out to Hollywood, where eight movies await him.

Apparently, Elvis is still the most.

Sincerely Elvis Presley

Elvis' gold suit gained much attention during his 1957 tours.

L.A. Police Order Presley 'Clean Up' His Pan-Pac Show

"Clean it up and tone it down."

That was the crisp order issued by L.A. police last night prior to the second and last Elvis Presley performance at the Pan-Pacific Auditorium. [This] came on the heels of the opening night performance which provided a chilling picture of Presley's impact on adolescent minds. Many sources flatly labeled the show "lewd," police reported. Others described it as the "most disgusting and most frightening" show they had seen.

However, city officials said that while the show probably was in "questionable taste," it did not violate any obscenity laws and no action was planned. But Deputy Chief Richard Simmons ordered his vice squad to give Presley strict orders that the alleged sexy stuff be cut.

Following last night's performance, Presley left immediately for his home in Memphis, for a two-month vacation before reporting back to Hollywood in January for another film assignment. He has just completed *Jailhouse Rock* for Metro and the film goes into release next month.

In Los Angeles, Elvis was ordered to clean up his act.

Elvis charms the press and fans backstage at the San Francisco Civic Auditorium before his concert on October 26, 1957. Calling his young fans, " Honey, " he often rubbed their shoulders and necks while talking to them.

KING CREOLE ★★★

Two years ago, Presley on the screen was a laughing stock. But nobody's laughing now. After that abysmal beginning—in *Love Me Tender*—the boy goes from length to strength. And this film hits the perfect formula for Elvis. That isn't to say it's a perfect film—far from it: just that it's perfect for Presley.

The setting is the steamy, sleazy tough quarter of New Orleans, in which the indolent intensity of Presley seems right at home.

And to match the atmosphere, the production is fast-paced, vicious, with a beat as insistent as the most vigorous rock 'n' roll.

The producer, Hal Wallis, has surrounded his star with players—notably Carolyn Jones, Dean Jagger, Paul Stewart—some of whose excellence and experience can't fail to rub off on Presley.

The grimy plot has him as a disgruntled teenager, who flunks his graduation and gets mixed up with thugs, racketeers and a good-hearted bad girl (Carolyn Jones). Inevitably, nightclub manager Paul Stewart discovers Presley has a voice: and naturally the customers go for it.

His down-at-heel father (Dean Jagger) disapproves and not even the love of a good woman (Dolores Hart) can prevent Presley from getting deep in trouble with a sadistic gang leader (Walter Matthau).

The story's hokum, but it's put over with a knowing air and acted with spirit; while a couple of the songs are better-than-average Presley. With this kind of backing there seems no reason why, after his army stint, he shouldn't become the big screen personality I thought he couldn't be.

Danny Fisher	ELVIS PRESLEY
Ronnie	CAROLYN JONES
Nellie	DOLORES HART
Mr. Fisher	DEAN JAGGER
"Forty" Nina	LILIANNE MONTEVECCHI
Maxie Fields	WALTER MATTHAU
Mimi Fisher	JAN SHEPARD
Charlie	PAUL STEWART
Shark	VIC MORROW
Sal	BRIAN HUTTON

Paramount American. "A." 116 minutes. Producer: Hal Wallis. Director: Michael Curtiz. Photographed by Russell Harlan. Screenplay: Herbert B. Baker and Michael Vincente Gazzo. From a novel, *A Stone For Danny Fisher*, By Harold Robbins. Release: September 21.

Back in Hollywood, Elvis wins over a new fan-actress Sophia Loren.

Elvis cozies up to costar Carolyn Jones on the set of King Creole.

'KING CREOLE' Offers Elvis—Little Else

"King Creole"

Produced by Hal B. Wallis, directed by Michael Curtiz, from a novel *A Stone for Danny Fisher*, by Harold Robbins, released by Paramount Pictures, and presented in the Chicago Theater.

THE CAST

Danny Fisher	Elvis Presley
Ronnie	Carolyn Jones
Nellie	Dolores Hart
Mr. Fisher	Dean Jagger
"Forty" Nina	Lilianne Montevecchi
Maxie Fields	Walter Matthau
Mimi	Jan Shepard
Charlie LeGrand	Paul Stewart
Shark	Vic Morrow

This shoddily produced film offers Elvis Presley and little else.

The script is aimed at generating sympathy for the hero who is forced to live in a slum because his pappy lost everything after his mama died. He works after school in a night club, and while he's protecting a woman from the unwanted attentions of a customer, he gets in all kinds of trouble. Bad company leads him from the straight and narrow and there is plenty of violence plus a number of murders before it's all over. The action is, of course, well laced with Presley singing in his usual unintelligible fashion.

Customers were rather scarce on opening day but a group of girls tried to stir up some excitement with their senseless squealing every time their hero opened his mouth. This in turn evoked a couple of good-natured boos from a trio of young sailors who watched the proceedings disdainfully. Personally I was on the side of the navy.

King Creole was Elvis' most critically acclaimed film.

39

Memphis Press-Scimitar   December 12, 1957

'What's the Fuss About?' Elvis Asks as Fans Cry

Draft Notice Comes, Girl Moans: 'I Never Thought It'd Happen'

BY JAMES F. PAGE, JR.   *Press-Scimitar Staff Writer*

"Dream," sang Elvis, "dream when you're feelin' blue . . ."

"Does that draft notice make you blue?" someone cracked.

"Who—me?" grinned E. P.

And that's the way it is with Uncle Sam's new prospective soldier—"ready to go—glad it's now"—at 22.

It was early this morning at Graceland, and Elvis plus buddies were ready for bed after a night on the town—maybe one of his last for awhile.

"I don't know what all the fuss is about," he said, running a comb thru his hair. "I'm just a guy who makes music—no different from anybody else."

But to millions of teen-agers he is different—something special.

They proved it while Elvis was at the movie.

"I feel like crying," said one girl, and she wasn't alone.

Fans began to crowd their hero's front gate early—and they stayed late.

Elvis was drafted in December 1957 but was able to finish King Creole before being inducted in March 1958. Vernon (below) was proud of his son the soldier

December 27, 1957

Elvis Given 60-Day Draft Deferment

MEMPHIS, Tenn., Dec. 27 (INS)—Singer Elvis Presley received a 60-day draft deferment today because of movie-making commitments.

Milton Bowers, chairman of the 23-year-old Presley's draft board, said it had been unanimously decided to allow the delay so his Hollywood studio could complete a picture already arranged.

The studio had asked for an eight-week extension, claiming that it would lose approximately $300,000 if Elvis reported for induction on Jan. 20, as scheduled.

The draft board refused the Hollywood request but said the rock-and-roll singer would have to ask for the additional time himself. He thereupon wrote, "Not on my behalf, but so these folks will not lose so much money with everything they have done so far."

Presley claimed from the start that he wanted no special favors for himself. He had said, "I'll go where they want me, when they want me."

Army Sharpens Shears for Elvis

'Operation Haircut' Is On

FORT CHAFFEE, Ark., March 19 (UP)—The Army assured Elvis Presley fans today that their hero's debut as a soldier will be fully publicized from blood tests to haircut.

The change from blue suede shoes to combat boots will be as fully documented as any other historical event.

Realistically admitting Pvt. Presley won't be "just another GI," the public information office here is preparing for his arrival on March 24 or 25 with enthusiasm usually reserved for approaching command inspections.

But "Operation Haircut" won't be the production one would expect. It seems Elvis accepted the inevitable and had his luxuriant growth sheared last week at his home in Memphis. His sideburns are gone.

However, the usual Army haircut and other induction ritual will be covered by the press.

Capt. Arlie Metheny, public information office, said yesterday a press center for visiting newsmen, photographers and television crews is being established.

"We got loads of letters from girls," Metheny said, **"who wanted us to save them a lock of Elvis' hair when he gets a GI haircut.**

"I hated to disappoint them, but we couldn't do it," he said.

"I issued a statement saying the hair will go in the trash with all the rest."

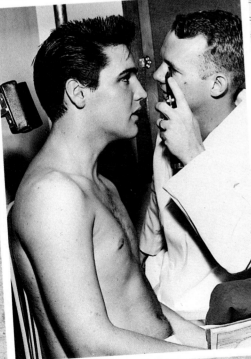

Top: Elvis' famous ducktail haircut was gone in a matter of seconds. Left: He's in the army now!

PRESLEY'S MOTHER DIES AT 42

MEMPHIS, TENN.—(UPI)—Mrs. Gladys Presley, 42, mother of singer Elvis Presley, died of an apparent heart attack Thursday only a short while after reporting she felt "so much better."

Presley, on a seven-day emergency furlough granted when his mother's liver ailment grew more serious earlier this week, was reported grief-stricken.

Mrs. Presley's husband, Vernon, was at her bedside in a local hospital when she died. Elvis who was asleep at his $100,000 suburban mansion "Graceland," arrived shortly after his mother's doctor had pronounced her dead.

* * *

THE SINGER, now as Army private stationed at Ft. Hood, Tex., was deeply attached to his mother. Friends said much of his devotion probably was a result of his twin brother's death at birth.

In achieving fame and wealth as a rock and roll entertainer, Elvis made good a promise made to his mother when the father was working as a Mississippi sharecropper and later when Elvis was driving a truck.

* * *

During her son's rise in the entertainment world, Mrs. Presley said very little in public, letting Elvis and her husband answer the questions of newsmen and the curious.

When the family moved from a $40,000 home in Memphis to the mansion, she commented. "I think I am going to like this new home. We will have a lot more privacy and a lot more room to put some of the things we have accumulated over the last few years."

Elvis was inconsolable upon the death of his mother, Gladys, in 1958. Shortly afterward, Pvt. Elvis Presley was stationed in Germany.

Life, March 14, 1960

The Army's Sergeant Elvis comes back home to girls he left behind him

In a spectacular shift of power that critically exposed the flank of U.S. music lovers the Army returned US53310761 from Germany last week for mustering out at Fort Dix, N.J. Fans mobilized to fighting strength and tuned up their shrieks. Mimeographed directives sped from the Pentagon as the Army proudly staged a press conference. Elvis was back.

After his two-year hitch, twenty-five-year-old rock 'n' roll idol Elvis Presley wore a sergeant's chevrons but no sideburns. "If I say the Army made a man of me," he said, "it would give the impression I was an idiot before I was drafted. I wasn't exactly that."

Elvis was, in fact, a smart soldier. His agents back home had been pretty smart too, selling 20 million RCA Victor records to the jukebox set. These earned "The Pelvis" $1.3 million in addition to his $145.24 a month service pay. Elvis paid the U.S. 91% of the total in taxes, or enough to support about 150 of his fellow soldiers for a year.

Behind him at Ray Barracks near Friedberg, Elvis had left hordes of palpitating Frauleins and the pretty 16-year-old Priscilla Beaulieu, daughter of an Air Force captain stationed at Wiesbaden. Elvis kissed her before he flew to the aid of the girls back home, sorrowful at parting but anxious to get into his bright-colored pants and back to his hip-swinging singing.

In press conferences after Elvis was discharged, reporters questioned him about Priscilla Beaulieu (below).

Communists Call Elvis Presley American Weapon In Cold War

BERLIN (UPI)—Communists are complaining about a new American weapon in the cold war named Elvis Presley.

The Communist youth newspaper "Young World" Saturday called Elvis a "Weapon in the American psychological war to infect a part of the population with the philosophical outlook of inhumanity . . . to destroy everything that is beautiful . . . to prepare for war."

He's public enemy no. 1, the Communists said, and western intelligence agencies are using him to recruit youths with "nuclear political views . . . for provocations."

The Red attacks on the gyrating singer followed a rock 'n' riot, at Chemnitz in East Germany. A group of rock 'n' roll fans who call themselves "The Presley Band" started the ruckus.

Seventeen youths have been arrested and police are seeking other ringleaders in the riot, Young World said.

The riot began in a square called the Scholssteich when teen-agers who gather there each night tuned their portable radios in on western stations which play the Presley records.

The people's police descended on the teen-agers and tried to confiscate the radios. The youths resisted and at first overpowered the police but reinforcements arrived and the youths were subdued.

$125,000 GUEST SHOT

Well, if Elvis Can Do It . . .

by Terry Turner

WHEN ELVIS Presley, a soldier, appears on a Frank Sinatra ABC-TV special in a few months, he'll receive a record payment for a guest appearance.

Elvis, tagged by some TV writers as "Our Leader," will receive $125,000.

Of course, you realize that Elvis will have expenses. He has to pay his manager and other people out of that salary. He won't be able to keep more than $100,000 or so. And then the government will step in to take a huge chunk.

* * *

NOBODY KNOWS, yet how long Elvis will be on camera when he appears with Sinatra. These are details that will be worked out later.

But assume he's on camera for half an hour.

He'll be making more than $4,000 a minute.

See, kiddies? Work hard, practice long hours, be blessed with talent. And you, too, may make $4,000 a minute one of these days.

(Who's bitter? I'm not bitter.)

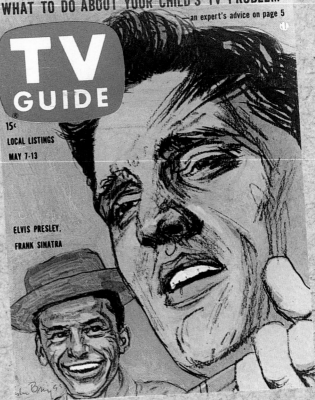

WHAT TO DO ABOUT YOUR CHILD'S TV PROBLEM
—an expert's advice on page 5

TV GUIDE

15¢
LOCAL LISTINGS
MAY 7-13

ELVIS PRESLEY,
FRANK SINATRA

Elvis' appearance on Frank Sinatra's TV special gained him acceptance with an older audience.

Memphis Commercial Appeal

Presley Sales Spin To Tune Of 76 Million

Elvis Presley was paid tribute yesterday for reaching the 76-million mark in record sales.

A plaque revealing Elvis' astounding achievement was presented to the Memphis singer yesterday at the $100-a-plate luncheon in his honor at the Claridge.

Two minutes after the announcement by George R. Marek, vice president and general manager of RCA Victor records, it was revealed that since the plaque was inscribed the latest Presley record has passed the million mark in sales. Elvis' latest record is "Surrender."

RCA also presented the Memphis singer-actor with an assortment of awards for record-breaking record sales in foreign countries.

The awards were for record sales in Australia, Belgium, Brazil, Denmark, England, France, Germany, Japan, The Netherlands, Norway, Sweden, and the Union of South Africa.

"It's Now or Never" heads the list with an old number, "Jailhouse Rock." Brazilians also like "It's Now or Never" and the favorite Presley disk in Japan is the same. In fact, this song heads the list of bestsellers or is a close second in most of the foreign countries.

Other awards presented to Elvis yesterday included the American Bandstand TV program for the "best male vocalist" in 1960 and Billboard magazine's award for disk jockeys' selection of "It's Now Or Never."

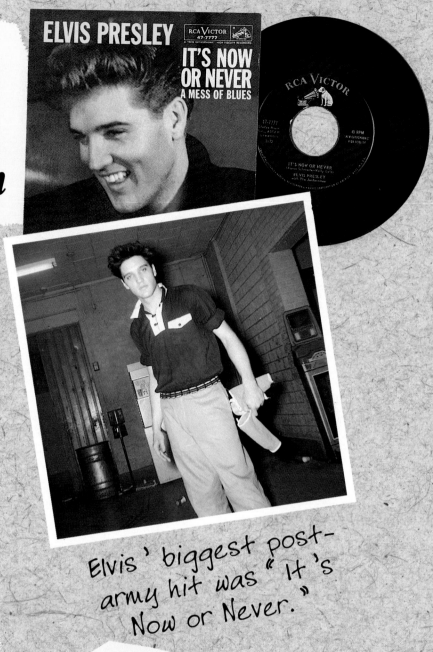

Elvis' biggest post-army hit was "It's Now or Never."

TV Guide

Elvis Comes Marching Home

By ALAN LEVY

Next Thursday (May 12), two generations of idolatry will be embodied on the television screen, when the 44-year-old son of a Hoboken boilermaker play host to a 25-year-old native of a "shotgun shanty" in Tupelo, Miss.

Ex-bobby-soxers—who once risked truancy to venture within swooning distance of "The Voice"—will watch their idol nostalgically and view with parental alarm their daughters' raptures over "The Pelvis." The men of their houses will gaze at either millionaire and ponder the classic riddle: "What's he got that I haven't got? . . ."

SCREEN IN REVIEW:

Presley Updated For His Comeback

Elvis was gone but not forgotten from 1958 to 1960. His astute manager, Col. Tom Parker, saw to that.

The comeback film, *G.I. Blues,* is designed to show what a model soldier he was around Frankfurt on the Main. It isn't all biographical. The plot idea is lifted from the 1933 Kenyon Nicholson play, *Sailor Beware!* which has not been purged of all impurities for Mr. Presley's teenage following. Recent surveys of the age group, however, disclose that only their elders are surprised at what their children are not surprised at.

With obscene hip-wiggle eliminated and hair trimmed to country club length, Elvis is an obedient draftee and a whizz at special services. He has an on-limits, off-hour combo for entertainment and sings at least uncredited 10 ditties of the type for which he is renowned. When not otherwise engaged he is the nicest guy on the post. He espouses the glacial Juliet Prowse (gratefully remembered from *Can-Can*) to save a bet for a pal. They fall in love, but she becomes indignant when she hears she is a game, then forgives when she looks in Elvis' bovine eyes.

He baby-sits for another buddy who has gone off to marry the infant's German mother. But as we said, teenagers are not even bewildered by such notions. Hal Wallis has given *G.I. Blues* a slightly self-conscious production, aware, doubtless, that Elvis Presley is social influence second only to hard drink. Norman Taurog's practiced hand was in the direction, making tolerable many digressions such as a scenic ride on the historic river.

On the set of G.I. Blues, Elvis waits for his cue (above) and receives a visit from Thai royalty (below).

46

BEHIND THE SCENES:

Is This a 'New' Presley?

The twelve pretty starlets had been shooed away from the vicinity of the great man in the shower for fear they would be a disturbing influence. The shower had been started, with cold water that would not streak his make-up, and the fake steam had been turned on. Then the pre-recorded music began and, in the latest switch on Hollywood's famous star-in-the-bath scene, Elvis Presley started mouthing "What's She Really Like?"—one of the eleven songs he sings in Paramount's "G.I. Blues."

In his first movie after two Army years in Germany, ex-Sergeant Presley was playing, of all things, a soldier stationed in, of all places, Germany. The sideburns and 15 pounds of flesh were gone, but otherwise it was just like the old days—oceans of hubbub washing over the star who, as long as he wasn't singing, remained quiet, deferential, and serious.

After the shower scene, Elvis changed into uniform and walked toward his luxurious dressing room several blocks away, answering, "Yes, sir," or "No, sir" to the questions put to him by underlings along the way. He strolled through an anteroom where half a dozen young men lounged in sports clothes—some of the nine pals he had brought from Memphis to Hollywood in a private railroad car (the trip cost him $2,424). The friends were variously carried on the payroll as "valet," "security guard," and "accountant." ("He was a bookkeeper before he went in the Army," Elvis says defensively of this last functionary.)

"If you don't mind, sir, I'll just keep my hat on while I eat," Elvis said, glancing at the air conditioner in his dressing room. "I got to keep this hair in place and I might catch a chill after that shower."

Mum on Show Biz: He began munching an unbuttered roll ("A lunch makes me sleepy") as he was asked about his Army stint. "I learned a lot about people in the Army," he said. "There was all different types. I never lived with other people before and had a chance to find out how they think. It sure changed me, but I can't tell you offhand just how. . . ."

"I never griped. If I didn't like something, nobody knew, excepting me. Nothing bad happened. If I'd 'a' been what they thought, I'd have got what was coming to me. But I never talked about show business. I went along."

He was asked about his future plans. "I'm ambitious to become a more serious actor, but I don't want to give up the music business by no means," he said. "I can't change my style, either. If I feel like moving around, I still move. As for the fans, they've changed some but they're still there, the same ones. The president of one fan club came to see me and I hardly recognized her. She's going to college now. I was surprised she looked me up. She was more mature, but she stopped by anyway."

Then the door burst open and a huge platter of tuna-fish sandwiches was borne in, followed eagerly by the pals.

SWING OUT AND SOUND OFF WITH
ELVIS PRESLEY
In the red, white and blue star-bright show of the year!
G·I·BLUES
A HAL WALLIS PRODUCTION
TECHNICOLOR
Directed by NORMAN TAUROG · Written by EDMUND BELOIN and HENRY GARSON · A PARAMOUNT RELEASE
JULIET PROWSE

Juliet Prowse costarred in G.I. Blues, which featured a new, more mature Elvis Presley.

ELVIS REMEMBERS PEARL HARBOR

Hawaii Next Charity Stop

By DON WALKER

When a 26-year-old ex-GI named Elvis Presley pays $100 to climb up on stage in Honolulu next March, twenty long and silent years will have passed for 1,102 American seamen entombed in the hull of the valiant battleship *Arizona*.

The average age of those shipmates who died during the Pearl Harbor disaster was about the same as that of the guitar-strumming singer who seeks to raise at least $50,000 towards a giant memorial to the *Arizona* crew and all who died for freedom.

Symbol of Freedom

The benefit performance by Presley—only a lad of five at the time war broke out—is symbolic of a new generation of Americans who have not forgotten the price of freedom or how dearly it has been maintained.

Except for the colossal charity benefit in his home-town of Memphis Feb. 25, the Honolulu public appearance will be Presley's first since he played the Hawaiian city in 1957 just prior to entry in the Army.

Filling the 4,000 seats of Pearl Harbor's Bloch Arena for the show, sponsored by the Pacific War Memorial Commission, will be a host of other Americans who will have contributed to the *Arizona* Memorial with the purchase of their tickets.

All For Arizona

All proceeds from the show will be channeled directly to the fund. Presley plans to buy the first ticket. His will cost $100. Everyone—top Navy brass, commission members and even Col. Tom Parker, Presley's manager who arranged the benefit, will pay. Though ticket costs will be scaled to meet the pocketbooks of all, a number of ringsiders will also pay $100 for their seats. A second performance will be added if the demand is great enough, Col. Parker said.

Parker Answers Plea

A Los Angeles newspaper's plea for help in raising the $200,000 still needed to complete the Memorial prompted Col. Parker to fly to Honolulu several weeks ago to offer Presley's service on the condition— "Every penny of that taken in must go to the fund."

H. Tucker Gratz, chairman of the Pacific War Memorial Commission, said the $50,000 anticipated from the benefit performance will provide "bare essentials" to prepare for the official dedication ceremonies on Memorial Day May 30. Since March 15, 1958 when Congress authorized the construction of the memorial museum through contributions, $300,000 has been raised. It was hoped that the final construction of the building would be completed by May 30, 1961—20 years after the murderous attack in which more than 3,000 Americans lost their lives.

A Proper Tribute

Presley and the Colonel responded to the commission's cry that fund collections had slowed to a snail's pace and "today the *Arizona* is but a rusting tomb . . . (while) the proposed memorial will be a proper tribute."

The commission hopes the Presley show will not only raise money itself but will also serve as a stimulus for obtaining the rest of the $200,000 necessary before the museum can become a reality.

Film To Follow

Col. Parker said Presley will arrive in Honolulu March 25 for the filming of *Blue Hawaii*. It will begin on March 27, the day after the benefit.

The giant museum building will stand on pilings—equal to the height of an 18-story building—over the Pacific near the hulk of the *Arizona*. One entire wall or bulkhead has been designed for the Honor Roll of the *Arizona's* crew, who hailed from all 48 states which then comprised the Union.

Elvis helped raise money for the U.S.S. <u>Arizona</u> Memorial in Honolulu by performing in a benefit concert.

Elvis family helps ease pair's grief

MEMPHIS, Tenn. (AP) — Elvis Presley's father and step-mother have helped ease the burdens of a Gleason [Tenn.] couple, beset by grief.

For seven weeks, Mr. and Mrs. Calvin Whitlow have kept a day-and-night vigil at a Memphis hospital where their 16-year-old son David, is ill with a brain tumor.

Monday, their home burned down, destroying their furniture, clothing and food.

Friday, Mr. and Mrs. Vernon Presley handed the Whitlows the keys to a station wagon crammed with food and clothing for them and six other children.

Mrs. Presley learned of the Whitlows and their ill son through a newspaper story and she visited them in the hospital.

"They told me then that their house burned down. I told Vernon and he ordered a turkey for the family for Thanksgiving."

Mrs. Presley also asked members of her church to help and they collected the food and clothing.

Vernon Presley bought the [brand-new] station wagon for the Whitlows so they could travel to Gleason to visit their other children.

Handing him the title to the vehicle, Presley said, "Here, Mr. Whitlow, good luck."

"May God bless Mr. Presley," Whitlow said.

Everything good
to all of you

Elvis
and
The Colonel

PEOPLE

Presley Gives $68,000 To Charity in 3 Cities

'Twas two days before Christmas and all through the day celebrities were giving and getting. . .

Elvis Presley, who made a fortune exercising in public, donated $68,000 to charities in Memphis, Tenn., Los Angeles, and Omaha, Neb.—a Christmas tradition he has followed for the past four years.

The 29-year-old Presley said he could remember when he wasn't a millionaire, and wanted to share his success with the needy.

Elvis remembered those who were less fortunate than he by contributing to charities each Christmas.

Angela Lansbury Quits Stage for Presley Film

By HEDDA HOPPER

Hollywood, May 15—An actress takes on mother roles when good parts run in that direction. Angela Lansbury who spent seven months on Broadway in *Taste of Honey*, and quit the production to play Elvis Presley's mother in *Blue Hawaii*, says: "In *Honey* I was the mother of Joan Plowright, a girl of 17 in the play; whereas Elvis is 26 and I admit it's a jolt for a woman of 35 to be asked to play his mother. It sort of stopped me, from the point of vanity. I thought—Do they think I'm that old? But the role intrigued me, it's a kind of comedy I'd never done before, a sort of grown-up baby doll and it takes me out of the British things". . . . Except for stars in series, she thinks TV has done little for run of the mill actors beyond giving them money to pay their bills. "A star like Richard Boone can make a fortune, and Lloyd Bridges has come up for air to count his money now. Actors reach the point where they feel they must provide some long-range security; so they do a series. An episode in a series, such as Have Gun, may have a cast of 20, but all except top stars and regulars on show get only the minimum pay and can work a series only once. . . ."

Hollywood columnist Hedda Hopper jokes with Elvis between takes.

Tuesday Weld charmed Elvis on and off the set of <u>Wild in the Country</u>.

WILD IN THE COUNTRY

You'd never recognize Elvis Presley as the singin' man of yore in this DeLuxe-colored saga of earthy Shenandoah Valley folklore. Without even a guitar he can call his own, Elvis does manage one wistful madrigal to a palpitating Tuesday Weld. The rest of the time Hope Lange, a psychiatrist, tries to bring out the best in Elvis, and Millie Perkins, ever on hand, just tries. Elvis, it would appear, has additional talent for writing. Whether this gift will ever have a chance to burgeon despite all the conflict with relatives, a murder charge, a suicide, and various other distractions is not for a woman to say. Instead, Elvis' future rests with John Ireland. In this emotional obstacle course, Elvis, in exceptional physical condition, seems hardly winded at all. (20th Century-Fox.)

Blue Hawaii, a colorful musical shot in America's 50th state, was Elvis' most successful film.

Elvis Presley Sings 'Blue Hawaii'

Elvis Presley is chipper and Hawaiian scenery is gaily colorful in *Blue Hawaii*. This new lure for the Presley hordes is showing at neighborhood theaters, all over town.

Elvis sings at the slightest excuse or none at all. Before he is through he has rolled up no less than 17 songs.

He mixes them up ranging through rock 'n' roll, ballads, Italian and Austrian songs and, of course, lots of Hawaiian music, both folk and "The Bird of Paradise" variety.

The story does not amount to much, a slender fable about the rich boy who wants to make good on his own instead of stepping into readymade success in his father's pineapple plant. The humor is equally inconsequential, most of it based on foolish misunderstandings, often on the vulgar side.

Elvis has two pretty girls for his dalliance, Joan Blackman and Nancy Walters. Angela Lansbury pops up again as a snobbish clown.

Except for the Hawaiian scenery and music, there is nothing in this one to distinguish it from all the other Presley movies since his return from the Army.

Blue Hawaii, with Elvis Presley, **Joan Blackman, Nancy Walters, Angela Lansbury, Roland Winters and John Archer. A Paramount film in color, directed by Norman Taurog, screen play by Ial Kanter, story by Allan Well. At neighborhood theaters. Running time: 1 hour, 41 minutes.**

FOLLOW THAT DREAM

WHO'S IN IT? Elvis Presley, Anne Helm, Arthur O'Connell, Joanna Moore.

WHAT'S IT ABOUT? As present-day home-steaders, a happy-go-lucky family has government authorities baffled.

WHAT'S THE VERDICT? Most of the way, it's a cheerful homespun comedy with easy-going songs and funny lines; so it can be forgiven for slowing to a near-standstill at the finish. Elvis, as a good-natured backwoods kid, and Anne, as a smart tomboy, make a romantic team that suits the picture's fresh approach.

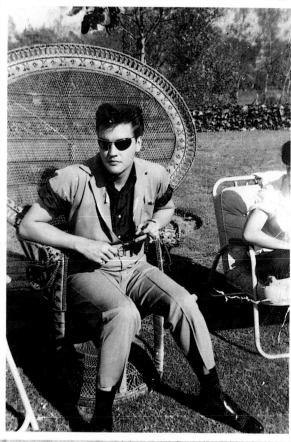

Elvis clowns around in these rare candids taken while on location in Florida for Follow that Dream.

52

More movies!
Fun in Acapulco (top);
Kid Galahad (middle); and
Kissin' Cousins
(bottom).

Elvis Presley Stars in 'Fun in Acapulco'

Elvis is back on the screen after an absence of several months, and his devotees should be ecstatic. Presley's new picture, called *Fun In Acapulco*, screens citywide.

In this musical movie, the young star sings about 10 times, but only once throws himself into the free-wheeling style that used to bring loud squeals from female teeners. A new "image"?

While plot and performances in *Fun In Acapulco* are about as substantial as the film's title, one can't dismiss the fact that producer Hal Wallis undoubtedly has another box office success. Presley buffs should eat it up.

Writer Allan Weiss places his hero in Acapulco, Mexico's plush resort, where he has been dismissed as seaman on a private yacht after refusing to romance the owner's daughter.

The young fellow secures work as a night club singer and life guard. In the latter capacity he hopes to overcome acrophobia, or fear of heights, which developed when he was a member of an aerial act involved in a fatal accident.

A romantic entanglement brings Elvis to the point of testing his phobia by subbing for one of the famous Acapulco high divers.

Director Richard Thorpe has kept the film's pace swift, which helps to cover up a lack of character development and a routine plot.

Two Heroines

Romantic interest for Presley is handsomely furnished by Elsa Cardenas and Ursula Andress. Paul Lukas, as an ex-duke turned chef, plays for comedy. Young Larry Domasin gives a lively portrayal of a kid who attaches himself to Elvis.

Alejandro Rey, Robert Carricart, Teri Hope and others enact supporting roles.

Memphis Commercial Appeal   November 8, 1963

Elvis Wins Love Of Ann-Margret

LONDON, Nov. 7—(UPI)—
Hollywood's Ann-Margret says she's going steady with Elvis Presley and "I guess I'm in love."

In London for the world premiere of the musical film "Bye Bye Birdie," the red-haired 22-year-old beauty said she doesn't know yet if they will get married.

"Nothing has been fixed," she said.

Ann-Margret said she and Elvis have lots of fun together riding motor bikes.

"I'm going steady with him and I guess I'm in love," she said. "But I cannot say when, or if, we will marry."

Added Ann-Margret: "He's a real man."

Ann-Margret heated up the screen as Elvis' costar in <u>Viva Las Vegas</u>. The two paired up behind the scenes as well.

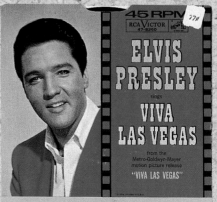

COMING SOON! SPECIAL "VIVA LAS VEGAS" EP • 4 NEW SONGS

ELVIS SWINGS IN— STILL ON TOP

…After 10 years Elvis Presley is a classical figure in rock 'n' roll, a respected institution—and still a howling success. Here, as a sheik, he swings into a harem in his new film, *Harem Holiday*. For 18 days' work in the movie he got $1 million plus 50% of profits. At 30, he is the highest paid actor in the world. In his decade at the top, Elvis has sold 100 million records, more than any other singer. He makes four single records a year and none sell less than 1,000,000.…

Elvis finds himself fascinated by Shelley Fabares, the bookworm coed he is supposed to chaperone.

M-G-M presents "GIRL HAPPY" Panavision® MetroColor

Copyright © 1965 Metro-Goldwyn-Mayer Inc.   Printed in U.S.A.

Elvis on the screen in
Girl Happy (top),
Harum Scarum (middle),
and *Roustabout* (bottom).

ROUSTABOUT

Paramount; Techniscope, Technicolor; Director, John Rich; Producer, Hall Wallis (Family)

WHO'S IN IT? Elvis Presley, Barbara Stanwyck, Joan Freeman, Leif Erickson
WHAT'S IT ABOUT? Set on staying footloose, a drifter gets entangled with a struggling small-time carnival.
WHAT'S THE VERDICT? The atmosphere of the midway livens up a Presley musical that has sturdier substance than his recent pictures. In keeping with his role, El looks tougher, more assured and more attractive. And it's good to see Barbara playing a sympathetic part for a change, as the carnival owner.

Elvis Grabs Cab, But First . . .

'I Touched Him,' Squeals Teener

HOLLYWOOD, April 21 (UPI)— It was a scene to warm the heart of the most hardened publicity man. Five-hundred squealing, giggling, sighing fans including a 72-year-old woman lined up last night to greet the return of their idol, singer Elvis Presley.

They gathered at Union Station hours before Mr. Presley and his entourage of nine friends were due to arrive aboard a private railroad car and patiently milled around when the train was almost an hour late.

'I TOUCHED HIM'

Although most of the fans were bypassed when Elvis' car was pulled to a siding where the young singer immediately boarded a taxi, one girl briefly touched him as he climbed into the cab.

"I touched him. . . . I touched him," she screamed as she dashed after the cab taking him to a hotel.

The 72-year-old fan who stood with the predominantly teenage crowd, identified herself as Mrs. Christine Rosen of Chicago and Los Angeles.

"I'm a fan of Elvis'," she said, tugging at the shawl around her shoulders. "But I don't dance rock and roll. . . ."

Top: A cab carrying Elvis navigates through a sea of fans. Right: Fan club paraphernalia for the devoted.

WHAT FANS THINK OF ELVIS

Anybody who doesn't like Elvis should see a doctor, because something must be wrong with them.

"Elvis Fan,"
Tarram, Vic.

If Elvis is a "has-been," why is it he wins the pop polls?

"The King Forever,"
Kilkivan, Qld.

If Elvis is a "has-been," how come he is so popular? I have heard of groups and singers whom people have said would last for years—but where are they now?

"Elvis Fan,"
Redwood Park, S.A.

I am an Elvis fan, always have been and always will be. At least he is always well dressed, with none of this long-haired sissy look.

"Angry Fredi,"
Adelaide City.

In reply to "Anti-Elvis," I say Elvis is the best performer on the pop scene today. His recordings are much more original and exciting than the Beatle-copiers, who comprise most of today's artists. His list of hits from 1956 to 1967 is a phenomenal one, which probably won't be equalled in our time.

"Another Teenager,"
Brisbane.

Elvis didn't need a gimmick like long hair to make him popular. He had—and still has—a style of his own. His popularity inevitably is shown in the number of films and recordings he has made.

"King of Kings Fan"
Reservoir, Vic.

Elvis is one pop star the whole family can enjoy.

"Elvis Forever,"
(a married woman),
Ballarat, Vic.

Elvis always takes time for photos and autographs for his fans.

A Tenderized Elvis Weds Longtime Gal Pal

Las Vegas, May 1 (AP)—Elvis Presley, the Mississippi boy who helped to popularize rock 'n' roll music and became a millionaire in the process, ended a reign as one of show business' most eligible bachelors today by marrying his longtime girl friend.

Presley, 32, and Priscilla Beaulieu, 22, took their vows before 14 friends in a hotel suite, then entertained 100 guests at a champagne breakfast. They said they will honeymoon for a month, probably somewhere in the United States.

Presley, who started in Memphis, Tenn., as a guitar-twanging, hip-wiggling singer, whose style has been widely imitated, has concentrated in recent years on movies. He came here from Palm Springs, Calif., for the ceremony.

Hotel Suite Ceremony

Nevada Supreme Court Justice David Zenoff performed the ceremony in the suite of Milton Prell, owner of the Aladdin Hotel. Best men were Presley's secretaries, Joe Esposito of Chicago and Marty Lacker of Memphis.

Presley wore a tuxedo. The bride, whose maid of honor was her sister, Michelle, wore a white chiffon gown embroidered with tiny pearls and full chiffon veil. Bodice and sleeves of her long train dress were of lace. She wore a 20-carat diamond ring with a three-carat centerstone, and carried a white Bible. The marriage was the first for both. Asked why he waited so long, Presley said: "Well, I guess it was about time. With the life I had, I decided it would be best to wait. You know, all of the shows and record engagements. . . ."

Hearts broke all over the world when Elvis married Priscilla Beaulieu on May 1, 1967, at the Aladdin Hotel in Las Vegas.

GIRL BORN TO PRESLEYS IN MEMPHIS

by
HARRISON CARROLL

It's a baby girl for film star Elvis Presley and his wife Priscilla Beaulieu.

The child was born at 5:01 p.m. yesterday in a Memphis hospital. She weighed 6-pounds 14-ounces. Both mother and child are doing fine.

According to Elvis they still haven't picked a name for the baby.

Presley is due back here in March to report to MGM for his next picture *Kiss My Firm But Pliant Lips.*

Lisa Marie Presley was born to proud parents Elvis and Priscilla on February 1, 1968.

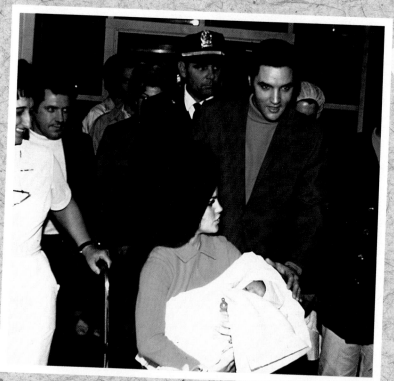

DAUGHTER BORN TO PRESLEY'S WIFE

MEMPHIS—Rock 'n' Roll star Elvis Presley became a father Thursday with the birth of a 6-pound 15-ounce girl Lisa Marie.

The baby was born at 5:01 p.m., 6 hours and 19 minutes after her attractive, brunette mother checked into Baptist Hospital. A hospital spokesman described Presley as "a pretty typical first-time father."

A DIFFERENT ELVIS?

Live a Little, Love a Little, MGM's latest Elvis Presley film, is, to say the least, a distinct departure for the former king of rock and roll.

For starters, Elvis sings just four songs. He's allowed to us a not inconsiderable comedic talent for the first time since Follow That Dream, and *Little* has a plot that serves as more than a device to change the scenery for the next production number.

The biggest surprise of all, though, is Michelle Carey, Elvis' co-star, nearly stealing the picture with a canny portrayal of Bernice, one of the kookiest girls ever put on film.

Part farce, part fantasy, *Little* now citywide, concerns a beach-dwelling, man-loving Miss Carey who isn't above sicking her dog on recalcitrant boyfriends.

The kind of girl who changes her name to suit her mood, she traps Elvis in her beach house, causes him to lose his job as a photo-journalist and moves him out of his home into one she likes better.

Thoroughly bewildered by her zany behavior, Elvis talks his way into two new full-time jobs with firms in the same building.

One is a sedate advertising outfit, the other a Playboy-type magazine. To keep both jobs, he scampers up and down a back stairway changing costume en route.

Desperately trying to make it with Bernice, but continually interrupted by either the dog or an old boy friend, Elvis gives up in frustration only to find Bernice not willing to give up on him.

He tries to date another girl but Bernice decides it's time to crack her head on a coffee table and confines herself to his bed. From there the film winds its way to an inevitable happy ending.

The supporting cast includes Don Porter, very funny in a take-off on Hugh Hefner's Playboy Philosophy; Rudy Vallee, injecting the correct amount of starch in his role as an advertising executive; Dick Sargent as Michelle Carey's boyfriend... and Joan Shawlee as a house wife who sees a potential molester behind every doorbell.

Little is extremely well-photographed, the special effects are finely executed and Billy Strange's score is Elvis's best.

Screenplayed by Michael A. Hoey and Dan Greenburg from Greenburg's novel, *Kiss My Firm But Pliant Lips*. *Live A Little, Love a Little* may just be the picture to finally break Elvis out of his static rock and roll mold.

Who wouldn't want to be Michele Carey in this scene?

Vernon Presley on the set of <u>Live a Little, Love a Little</u>

60

Presley pranks

Stay Away, Joe turns out to be sound advice to the public, though it's actually the title of the latest Elvis Presley movie which is by far the weakest he's made for some time.

The assumption seems to be that Presley doesn't need a story or much in the way of songs any more. Just gather a gang of pretty girls, rowdy men, and a few slapstick comedians, get out the color cameras, and let Presley strut through a few reels of wild parties and juvenile pranks. The result is a flat, forced collection of scenes that looks like the rejects from some other, better film.

Presley is the irresponsible son of a American Indian family who returns to the dilapidated homestead with a herd of government-supplied heifers and a bull. From the moment the welcome-home party begins (and it goes on for more than half an hour), it's clear that any plot considerations have been discarded in favor of a series of loosely related gags of the kind that used to be described as "zany hi-jinks."

The Indians are depicted as a grubby, shiftless lot, the performances of Burgess Meredith, Joan Blondell, Katy Jurado and Thomas Gomez are desperately antic, and Presley doesn't bother to act at all, he's just there.

The picture is just about as awful as a movie can get. One searches in vain for some redeeming feature but there is absolutely nothing to recommend.

J. M. I.

IT'S
ELVIS in "CLAMBAKE"
LEVY-GARDNER-LAVEN presents
TECHNISCOPE® TECHNICOLOR®

Clambake was Elvis' 25th movie in 11 years.

SPEEDWAY

Speedway is the latest release of one of the current top ten favorites, **Elvis Presley,** and the 26th film of his fantastic 11-year career. It is also his eighth for M-G-M who this time present him with two special gifts. One is sensational singing star **Nancy Sinatra** as his leading lady, and the other is an exciting story set in the daredevil world of stock car racing.

Elvis plays a top racing champ whose irresponsibility puts him heavily in debt with the income tax people. Nancy is an Internal Revenue agent assigned to follow Elvis around and get her hands on his money before he starts being rash with it. When the two are not involved in comedy, romance and racing, they share a series of tender ballads and fast-paced dance songs.

Racing sequences were shot at a famous speedway in North Carolina, and provide suspenseful spinouts and frightening crashes. More frenzied action takes place in a discotheque called The Hangout where the booths are made from cars. All in all, *Speedway* should please the Presley fans, of whom there are still many millions.

BRIAN SWIFT

Nancy Sinatra and Bill Bixby gave Speedway an added punch.

61

ELVIS

9:00 [20]

Special Color Surrounded by musicians and adoring fans Elvis Presley headlines his first TV special.

The fans are up and screaming as Elvis rocks through a nostalgic medley of his hits: "Heartbreak Hotel," "Hound Dog," "All Shook Up," "Can't Help Falling in Love with You," "Jailhouse Rock," and "Love Me Tender." He also sings "Memories" and his seasonal hit "Blue Christmas."

The Blossoms vocal group and dancer-choreographer Claude Thompson open a gospel medley with "Sometimes I Feel like a Motherless Child," and Elvis joins them for "Where Could I Go but to the Lord?" "Up Above My Head" and "Saved!"

A rocking production number stars Elvis as a traveling musician (singing "Guitar Man") who leaves a dull job ("Nothingsville") for an amusement park ("Big Boss Man") and modest night-club success ("Trouble"). Finale: "If I Can Dream," written for Elvis by vocal arranger Earl Brown. (60 min.)

Talented producer Steve Binder (second from left) was the creative center of Elvis' successful tv special.

ELVIS'

[NB] TELEVISION
special
Presented by
The SINGER Company
Tuesday, December 3, 1968

Tune in the outstanding event of the TV season!

SINGER
presents

ELVIS

*In his first
TV SPECIAL!*

TUES., DEC. 3rd
NBC-TV : IN COLOR
9PM EST/PST 8PM CST/MST

NA 5628

SINGER presents....

ELVIS!
NBC-TV / DEC.3 / 9 PM (EST)

Elvis Skips Gyrations but Still Generates Heat

So much rock 'n' roll has been performed in the past dozen years that Elvis Presley's doing his first special on TV Tuesday night somehow seemed anti-climactic—even though he was one of the pioneers in the field.

ELVIS

Elvis Presley in a musical special. Executive producer Bob Finkel. Producer-director Steve Binder. Writers Allan Bive, Chris Beard. Musical production Bones Howe. Musical direction and arrangements William Goldberg. Special lyrics and vocal arrangements Earl Brown. Choreographer Jamie Rogers, Claude Thompson. NBC Tuesday, 9 p.m.

The Elvis hour on NBC was virtually a one-man show with the star doing most of his numbers on a small square stage surrounded by a studio audience which had some screamers in it. But according to executive producer Bob Finkel, none of them were hand-picked. They just simply loved Elvis.

Although he didn't indulge in the dynamic physical gyrations which made him so controversial that we saw only the top half of him on an Ed Sullivan Show many years ago, Elvis still generates considerable heat with his singing.

His repertoire included many of his recorded hits such as "Hound Dog," "Jailhouse Rock" and "Love Me Tender." Producer-director Steve Binder employed lots of camera closeups and two-camera superimposed shots, which were effective, except for those closeups showing Elvis sweating. I don't think many viewers care to see singers sweat on TV.

Moving away from the small stage and studio audience, Elvis did two impressive production numbers. One was a gospel song with dancers and singers; the other opened on a carnival midway and progressed from his singing in a joint to better-class night-clubs.

The show closed with him in a white suit standing in front of the huge lit letters spelling E-L-V-I-S which opened the proceedings, and he sang "If I Can Dream."

Except for TV runs of his old movies, this marked Elvis' first TV appearance since he did a guest shot on a Frank Sinatra special in 1960, so it was an event in that sense and Elvis managed to sustain the hour very well.

Even so, as I said at the beginning, there was the feeling of anti-climax. Some of the magic was gone, diminished by the fact that this type of music has progressed and hotter names have come along since Elvis to perform it.

—HAL HUMPHREY

★★★★★★★★★★★★★★★★★★
MOVIE SCENE

by Frances Herridge

NEW PRESLEY MOVIE AT SHOWCASES

Elvis Presley's new film, *The Trouble With Girls,* has a lot more trouble than it seems to realize. You can't blame the cast, even the girls—though they're pretty bad. The main fault is the script.

It's a bland hodgepodge that mixes a seedy murder with tedious goings-on in a 1927 Chautauqua tent show. Presley as the show's manager is beset with problems—like whether to give the mayor's untalented daughter the lead in the children's pageant, how to deal with a pretty assistant who keeps bugging him about union rules, how to avoid an unfunny comedienne who pursues him, how to get his card player out of jail when he is accused of killing the town's villain.

These loose ends are sloppily tied together by one of those improvised stage shows which must keep going until the real murderer sobers up enough to confess. Seems forever.

THE TROUBLE WITH GIRLS

An MGM release. Produced by Lester Welch. Directed by Peter Tewksbury. Screenplay by Arnold and Lois Peyser from novel by Day Keen and Dwight Babcock. Cast includes Elvis Presley, Marlyn Mason, Nicole Jaffe, Sheree North, Edward Andrews and Vincent Price. 105 minutes.

There's nothing wrong with Presley. He wisely underacts, and sings pleasantly. But why doesn't he find better scripts—at least ones that give him more than three so-so songs.

The film is at showcase theaters with *Flare Up*—another loser.

Colonel Tom Parker on the set of *Change of Habit*

Charro! resembled an Italian western.

The Trouble with Girls featured 450 extras.

64

Elvis Helps Push Memphis Sound

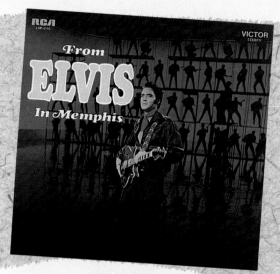

Left: Elvis updated his music with *From Elvis in Memphis*. Below: "Kentucky Rain" became a hit single in 1970.

Elvis Home— Cuts 16 Sides

MEMPHIS—Elvis Presley and a contingent of RCA recording technicians quietly slipped in here last week and recorded a 16-tune session at American Record Studios. In the only recording studio interview granted by Presley since he joined RCA he said,"This is where it all started for me. It feels good to be back in Memphis recording."

American, headed by Chips Moman, is regarded as one of the "hottest" studios today and responsible for such hits as "Hooked on a Feeling," by B.J. Thomas and "Son of a Preacher Man," by Dusty Springfield.

The session, from which an LP and singles will be produced, utilized American's studio band, a symphony orchestra string section, local brass men and a chorus.

Here from RCA's Nashville studios were Felton Jarvis, Al Pachuki and Roy Shockley, Harry Jenkins, vice-president, RCA's record division, New York, was also here.

Moman, co-owner of the studio with Bob Crews, manned the control board. Presley and Jarvis teamed with Moman in producing the session.

Presley said the session, his first since recording here on Sun Records in 1954, was the first that did not also involve motion pictures. "This is especially refreshing," he said.

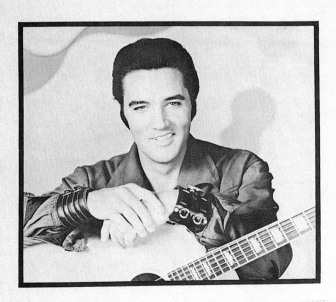

As Recorded by ELVIS PRESLEY on RCA Records

KENTUCKY RAIN

Words and Music by EDDIE RABBITT and DICK HEARD

PRICE $1.50 IN U.S.A.

ELVIS PRESLEY MUSIC, INC. and S-P-R MUSIC CORP.
SOLE SELLING AGENT:
HILL AND RANGE SONGS, INC.
241 West 72nd Street, New York, N.Y. 10023

Rock Music

Elvis: An Artistic Renaissance

LAS VEGAS—Elvis is back. He had been away.

Good music seems to be one thing that's left after life has moved on. Elvis Presley is a good musician, a great singer, and—quite possibly—the most magnetic performer in the history of (what's commonly called) show biz.

If there had never been an Elvis Presley, certainly no one could have invented him.

The emotional reaction to his first live appearance in nine years is akin to the way a St. Petersburg reporter described the chaotic aftermath of a Presley concert back in 1956: "The Pied Piper of rock 'n roll, a swivel-hipped, leg-lashing entertainment bomb, blasted the downtown area into chaos all day yesterday.

"Screaming, fainting teenagers lined the streets early to catch a glimpse of Elvis Presley, a rock-a-billy gyrating singer who's shattered show business with his sultry style. He hit St. Petersburg with the effect of a small H-bomb, sending fans into mass hysteria and receiving an ovation rarely seen on the Suncoast."

Elvis was the symbol of anti-establishment behavior before Mario Savio had left grade-school. Some suggested he was a Communist plot.

But for better or worse, he fathered a new art form in popular music called rock 'n roll.

Back in 1956, Presley was studying to be an electrician. But, he remembers, "I got wired the wrong way."

He caused a major squirmish when he appeared on the Ed Sullivan show. Then he went to Hollywood.

"My first movie ('Love Me Tender') was kind of weird." But he persevered. "I made four more movies and then I got drafted."

When Elvis returned from the service, something had changed. The taut, casually sinister figure had rounded out. The exuberant spirit seemed to have atrophied. And his singing had become too jello-smooth for its own good. He went through an artistic Dark Age.

In his own words, "I got hung up in Hollywood, making pictures and got away from the people."

But now he is back.

Same swivel-hips. Same gyrations. Same emotional strangle-hold.

His victims are now 30-plus. Hardened waitresses, who just recently struggled through the ennuied debut of the Divine Barbara, were visibly swooning. A well-attired matron scrambled on stage without once breaking stride and corralled the shy Presley.

And his artistry is undiminished. In fact, it seems even enhanced when compared to the rather-trendy impulse by some "to return to the roots of rock 'n roll."

When Elvis swings into "Blue Suede Shows," and "I Got a Woman," and "All Shook Up," and all the others he is where it is at. That's one of the few truths in pop music.

Elvis reflects for a moment during his Vegas press conference.

Elvis and Priscilla pal around with Tom Jones (center).

In 1969, Elvis returned to the stage with a vengeance.

A LEGEND THAT LIVES

By FRANK LIEBERMAN

LAS VEGAS—At the airport, the International Hotel's towering marquee simply reads "ELVIS."

The cab drivers ask, "Are you going to see Elvis?"

Patrons at every hotel are talking about seeing or trying to see Elvis.

Elvis Presley, now a legend, is alive.

He's the ghost who walks on the stage of the International showroom twice nightly to capacity throngs of 2000-plus per show. Never in the annals of Las Vegas show business has an entertainer caused such a clamor.

But there has never been another Elvis Presley.

Few guests, if any, leave the International disappointed. Presley's life-long ambition is to make people happy, to entertain them, to become a friend. He would like to get out and meet them all.

Elvis Presley, to the people, is "The King."

Presley's nine-year hiatus from clubs ended last August. It gave his fans a new chance to view their idol. What so many people don't realize is that it did more for the man himself.

"It gave me a new life. I was human again," Presley said in his International dressing room. "There was hope for the future. New things, new ways. It wasn't the same old movies, the same type of songs. I was able to give some feeling, put some expression into my work.

"And it gave me a chance to do what I do best, sing," added Elvis, with a smiling, friendly "let's cut out that bragging," look.

Presley is 35 now, and happily married, despite rumors to the contrary. His 6-foot plus thin frame stands tall and his pitch-black hair is still long. But the shyness and self-conscious slouch that always were associated with the younger Presley are gone.

On his fingers are four rings, all gleaming despite the lack of light in the dressing quarters.

Presley's clothes are "in," but not outlandish. On stage he wore white. Relaxing, he wore black.

The country boy image has vanished. His coterie has been reduced to four or five instead of the old 10 to 13. And those left are friends and workers. The body-guard front is no longer.

His words are clear and precise, the old cornpone accent barely discernible. His return to the stage is a giant step forward.

Following his first engagement, Presley returned to this city as a tourist. He was seen kissing admirers, signing autographs, playing blackjack, and doing the things ordinary people do.

His newest movie, "Change of Habit," came and went, just as the star was doing from hotel to hotel. It didn't matter, for Elvis was doing what he wanted. He wasn't hiding and sneaking about. No walks through kitchens, up back elevators. He was Elvis Presley, a human being . . . .

His stage comeback made him a legend.

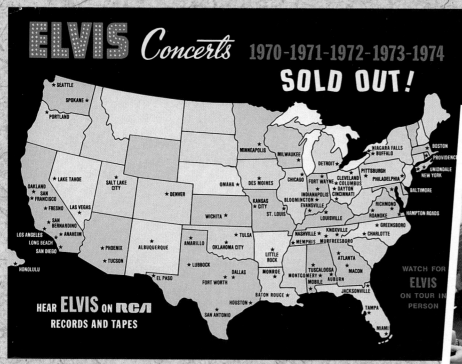

Shortly after his second Vegas success in 1970, Elvis returned to the road.

ELVIS— HE'S BACK!

Elvis Presley has starred in 31 motion pictures. Number 32 is both a unique project for Presley and an unusual approach to movie entertainment. For the first time Elvis is seen on film as he really is, portrayed as an artist and as a phenomenon.

MGM's "Elvis . . . That's The Way It Is" was directed by two-time Academy Award-winner Denis Sanders, who explains, "The subject is Elvis and the core of the picture is Elvis on stage in Las Vegas performing his incredible, record-breaking act."

Sanders continues, "However, we went much further with the cameras. We attempted to capture the ups and downs he experiences putting his show together, showing the man as a musician. We filmed both sides of the lights, exploring what he feels and the emotions he creates in others."

Pursuing that goal, the director photographed his subject in private rehearsals at MGM Studios, further rehearsals in Las Vegas and then on stage in the Showroom Internationale of Las Vegas' International Hotel. MGM cameras were also on hand in Phoenix, September 9, for the opening of the star's first concert tour in thirteen years.

To gain insight into Presley's following, certainly the largest and most varied group of fans in entertainment, Sanders interviewed businessmen, students, housewives and a bride, among others, in settings ranging from living rooms to churches, talking with a variety of people who have literally devoted varying proportions of their existence to the former teenage truck driver named Elvis Presley. Additionally, he travelled to Europe to capture the Fifth Annual Elvis Presley Appreciation Society Convention, attended by up to 4,000 people of all ages each year in Luxembourg.

Elvis pours it on in the 1972 documentary Elvis on Tour.

Elvis rehearses in the 1970 documentary Elvis—That's the Way It Is.

69

Jaycees Urged To Get In Arena

A hectic day of Jaycee activities yesterday was highlighted by a luncheon speech from United Nations Ambassador-appointee George Bush and last night by the organization's awards ceremony honoring the Ten Outstanding Young Men in America.

The slender, Texas oil millionaire, whom many believe was President Nixon's United Nations choice because he ran gamely but unsuccessfully for the Senate seat held by Ralph Yarborough, spoke to an estimated 1,100 at the Holiday Inn-Rivermont.

He praised his audience as "men who have thought new thoughts and rejected old dogmas. But to guarantee this country never accepts the violent answer," our people must be willing to work "within the system," he said.

He complimented the Jaycees on their "Top Ten" selection and told Memphis politicians to "watch out" if entertainer Elvis Presley ever decided to enter politics. "They would have to regroup their forces," he said.

Last night at the awards ceremony the entertainer had a few words for the 2,000 persons at the Auditorium.

"I've always been a dreamer. When I was young I used to read comic books and go to movies, and I was the hero.

"My dreams have come true a 100 times over. These men here," he said, pointing to the nine other award winners, "they care. You stop to think, and they're building the kingdom of heaven."

Dressed in a modest black tuxedo, Elvis closed by saying that without a song the day never ends. "So I just keep singing a song," he said as tears rushed to his eyes.

The singer had one hand too few as he accepted the award from the United States Jaycee President Gordon Thomas. Shaking Mr. Thomas' hand and taking the Outstanding Man trophy in the other, Elvis had no place to hold his yellow "Easy Rider" sunglasses.

Each of the Outstanding Men made a short speech prior to receiving their awards.

Thomas Atkins, Boston's first black councilman, called on Jaycees throughout the country to donate one dollar per year for four years to advance the ideals of the late Dr. Martin Luther King.

"I appeal to you to lift this country from the quicksand of racism to the solid rock of human dignity," Mr. Atkins said.

Wendell Cherry, president of Extendicare Nursing Corp., in his address said the American system will continue to work as long as people such as the Jaycees continue to involve themselves in community life.

"We must temper our urge to overcome with compassion and patience," he said. Then quoting Tennyson, he closed with, "Come my friend, 'tis not too late to seek a newer world."

Comic strip artist Al Capp, was scheduled to be master of ceremonies at the awards ceremony but did not appear.

"He wasn't able to come due to a last minute breakdown in communications," said Ken Scrivner, public relations director of the Jaycees. He declined to elaborate on Mr. Capp's absence.

Ron Zeigler, White House press secretary, paid tribute to the Jaycees for accepting "the high adventure of being Americans.

"This nation has a history of striving, stretching, doing and caring. We have refused to believe that things are impossible," he said.

Others honored were Dr. Mario Capecchi, a biophysicist at Harvard Medical School; Dr. George Todaro, researcher for the National Cancer Institute; Capt. Paul William Bucha, professor at West Point; Walter J. Humann, corporation executive; Jim Goetz, radio station owner; and Thomas Edward Coll, founder of a private volunteer service.

Mr. Bush earlier praised Presley's comments at the morning forum, closed to the press, in which Jaycees attending the 33rd congress were permitted to question the honorees.

In that forum, Elvis "held his own" with his more "learned colleagues," said George Cajoleas, president of the Bradenton, Fla., Jaycees.

"He was forthright in his answers and didn't stumble. The guy came off looking very good, although he seemed very humble. I felt he was very impressed with the men around him in terms of their contributions to social advancement."

The honorees were asked if they made a religious commitment before undertaking their life's work.

"Six or seven of the men said they didn't belong to a church and felt a certain hypocrisy about organized religion. But Elvis seemed to feel religion was very important in his life, not in the organized sense, but in the sense that he had called on God many times for strength. I think he also quoted some scripture," said Mr. Cajoleas.

Presley said after the luncheon that he didn't quote scripture but had "commented that God is a living presence in all of us."

Elvis clutches his award from the Jaycees.

MEMPHIS, Tenn., Jan. 16—PRESLEY AND WIFE AT PRAYER BREAKFAST—Elvis Presley and his wife stand for their introduction Saturday morning at a U. S. Jaycees prayer breakfast. Presley is one of Ten Outstanding Young Men being honored here by the Jaycees. The Memphis entertainer wore a fur suit for the breakfast and later appeared at a forum with the other winners. Award ceremonies were Saturday night.

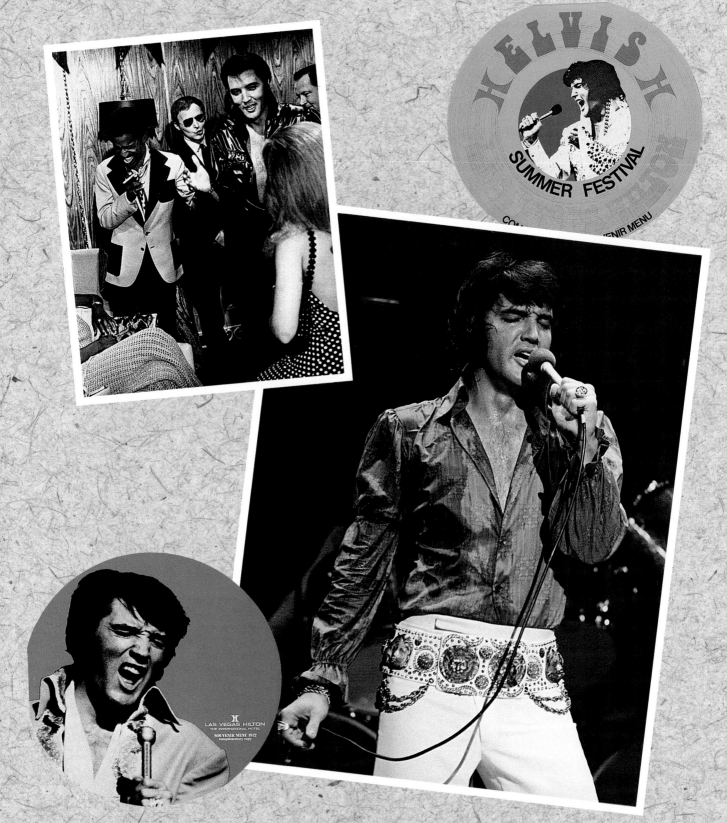

Elvis performed for a month each summer and winter at the Las Vegas Hilton. He became pals with the Vegas crowd, including Sammy Davis, Jr.

Elvis takes a hefty bite out of the Big Apple!

PRESLEY'S NEW YORK DEBUT

In the star spangled, legendary career of Elvis Presley the impossible has become an accomplishment at every turn. Yet in the 17 odd years that his career has raged he had not, until a few weeks ago played in the largest city of the U.S.—New York.

Presley made his New York debut at Madison Square Garden. Outside that concrete colosseum there were traffic jams that caused half of New York to grind to a halt. Inside, there were guys selling Elvis posters, Elvis buttons, Elvis LP's and Elvis everythings.

The orchestra played "2001: Space Odyssey" and Presley ran on stage accompanied to the edge by four bodyguards. His suit was white with a red stripe down each side of the trouser legs.

He opened with "That's Alright," then "Proud Mary," "You Don't Have to Say You Love Me," and "Believe Me." The Sweet Inspirations were there as backing chorus, plus a group and the orchestra—they all suffered from technical difficulties. No-one on that vast stage really got it together.

"Polk Salad Annie," "I've Never Been to Heaven," "Love Me Tender," "Heartbreak Hotel," "All Shook Up"—the crowd reactions varied from song to song but the biggest explosion was for "Hound Dog." In this, Elvis started real slow, building to its normal fast tempo with the full beat, gyrations and all.

Elvis' concerts at Madison Square Garden in 1972 represented his NYC debut.

Presley's career still going strong

United Press International

NEW YORK—Elvis Presley said yesterday his gyrating performances of 15 years ago, which shocked thousands of parents and got him censored below the waist on television, were "tame compared to what they're doing now."

"All I did was jiggle," Presley, now 37, said during one of his rare news conferences.

Appearing with his father, Vernon, Presley was greeted by the usual feminine screams on the eve of his first appearance in New York City.

"I love you, Elvis," shouted an attractive woman reporter in her mid-20s. "Thank you, dear," replied Presley.

Asked about the screams which started more than 15 years and 30 gold records ago, Presley said, "I got used to them. I'd miss it now if it didn't happen. To me, it's part of the business and I accept it."

Wearing a baby blue coat with a long, flowing dark blue cape, Presley was asked the reason for the length of his career. "I take Vitamin E," he quipped.

But he added, "I don't know. I enjoy the business.

"I'd like to think I've improved over the last 15 years," he said. "But I don't want to take away from my early hits. I'm not the least bit ashamed of 'Hound Dog' and 'Heartbreak Hotel.'"

Presley, whose weekend appearances at Madison Square Garden reportedly were sold out in record time, also was asked his views on Vietnam and politics.

"Honey," he replied to the female reporter asking the questions, "I'd just as soon keep my personal opinions to myself. I'm just an entertainer."

Silver-haired Vernon Presley then got into the act. He was asked by another woman reporter what he thought of his son's success.

"Kinda hard to say," replied the elder Presley, "Happened so fast—boom—in 1956 after the first (Ed) Sullivan Show."

Elvis

You say you attended the recent Elvis Presley concert and you wish you could experience again that night of rapture? Now, for you, thru the magic of rush releasing—and even before your photos get back from the drugstore—RCA presents "Elvis —As Recorded at Madison Square Garden." The Garden performance was part of the same tour that brought Presley to Chicago, and the shows were essentially the same, from the "Also Sprach Zarathustra" intro to the encore-stifling "Elvis has left the building." In between, El does a healthy 47 minutes or so of oldies like "Heartbreak Hotel" and newies like "American Trilogy."

The Garden concert, incidentally, was held on June 10. The record was ready about two weeks later. Pretty soon, folks, they'll have 'em on sale as you file out the door.

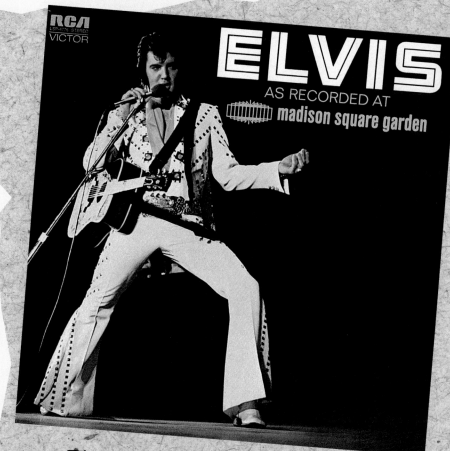

The LP from the Garden concerts was recorded, mixed, pressed, and released to the stores in less than two weeks

Elvis Sues Wife for Divorce

LOS ANGELES, Aug. 19 (AP) —Entertainer Elvis Presley sued his wife of five years for divorce Friday, citing irreconcilable differences.

The suit, filed by one of Mr. Presley's attorneys in Santa Monica Superior Court, conceded that his wife, Priscilla, 24, will have custody of the couple's daughter, Lisa, 4.

In the suit, Mr. Presley said a major reason for the divorce was the pressure of his traveling half the year.

Mr. Presley, 37, and his wife were reported to have reached agreement on a property settlement, but the terms have not been made public.

July 27, 1972

Discordant note for Elvis?

A Memphis newspaper reports that millionaire singer Elvis Presley and his wife Priscilla have separated. She reportedly has left the Memphis mansion and moved to Los Angeles with their 4-year-old daughter.

After five years of marriage, Elvis and Priscilla divorced in 1972, but the pair remained friends.

Elvis blamed
his life on
the road
for the
breakup of
his marriage.

Elvis' 'Aloha From Hawaii' Is First Number One Quad Album

NEW YORK—The Elvis Presley RCA album, "Elvis, Aloha from Hawaii-Via Satellite," hit number one on the charts last week, thus becoming the first compatible quad record ever to become a nation-wide number one hit, less than a year after RCA's entry into the quad market.

The two-record album, of which almost one million sets have been sold in America alone, previously had become the first quad album ever to be certified as a million-dollar gold Album by the Recording Industry Association of America . . . .

Elvis: Aloha from Hawaii was eventually seen by 1.5 billion people.

T.V. GUIDE   MARCH 31-APRIL 6, 1973

**ELVIS: ALOHA
FROM HAWAII**
8:30 ③

Special: Elvis Presley is in top form for this Hawaiian concert.

Backed by shifting light patterns and scenes of lush Oahu, Elvis delivers 90 minutes of songs including his hits "Blue Suede Shoes," "Hound Dog," "Blue Hawaii," "Can't Help Falling in Love," "Suspicious Minds," "All Shook Up," and "Burning Love."

Highlighting the rest of the concert: "Early Morning Rain," "My Way," "Fever," "I'll Remember You," "Welcome to My World," "I'm So Lonesome I Could Cry," "Johnny B. Goode," "C.C. Rider," "What Now, My Love?" and a medley of patriotic songs.

The musical backing is by J.D. Sumner and the Stamps, Kathy Westmoreland, Sweet Inspirations and the Joe Guercio Orchestra.

The program was taped in January at the Honolulu International Center.

Elvis stirs up nets

HOLLYWOOD—This must be a first: an entertainment special that will be aired on NBC considered so important, news teams from both competing networks are requesting permission to cover its production.

The special event is the Elvis Presley concert that's going to be beamed live from Honolulu via GlobCom satellite on Jan. 14 to countries around the world, and recorded by NBC for American viewing in February.

What's creating all the interest is not the fact that this will mark Elvis' first turn on the tube since 1969—but that it will be the first entertainment show ever to utilize satellite transmission.

Even M-G-M is attempting to cash in on the publicity the broadcasting first is generating.

The studio, in conjunction with producers Bob Abel and Pierre Adige, has pulled the "Elvis on Tour" documentary out of its theatrical run, and is planning its re-release to coincide with Presley's concert-by-satellite.

"Elvis on Tour" already has recouped its negative cost with limited playdates in the South and a few Midwestern states, so it's clear profits from here on in—particularly healthy profits, they figure.

Elvis loved Hawaii, both as a vacation spot and as a place to work. Here fans welcome him at the airport as he arrives to do Elvis: Aloha from Hawaii.

Elvis moves hips—

Bill Belew designed many of Elvis' jumpsuits, which were an array of colors and patterns.

Screams fill Chicago Stadium

THE ALL-TIME KING of rock and roll made his second appearance in history in Chicago last night and all passed peacefully.

Elvis Presley, now 37, stepped out on the stage of the Chicago Stadium to an ocean of screams and a fantastic explosion of flash bulbs from 20,000 fans who had gathered to hear him sing oldies and newies and watch him swivel those hips.

The crowd ranged from infants to grandmothers. Most were conventionally dressed. A large contingent of Andy Frain ushers were on hand and Presley's own traveling security force patrolled the fringes of the stage, which was set up on the west side of the stadium floor. But there was no trouble.

THREE TIMES DURING the performance, Presley made sojourns to the three sides of the stage, touching arms and tossing his gold scarves to the crowd. At one point, a brassiere was thrown at his feet. He picked it up, regarded it tenderly and placed it on his head before throwing it to the floor.

Fans continued to throw handkerchiefs, pictures, candy and keys to the stage, but Presley ignored the barrage and performed his nonstop, nearly hour-long act.

PRESLEY'S FANS have changed in the years since his 1957 appearance here in the International Amphitheater, but his appeal has endured. Girls who were not yet born at that time, screamed and jumped on their seats throughout the concert.

"My God," one young lady said as Presley swung into his old hit, "Heartbreak Hotel," "I was two when he recorded that."

Tickets for the concert, the first of three in two days here, ranged from $10 down. The box office receipts were estimated at upwards of $150,000 for last night's concert. Tonight's affair is sold out.

CHICAGO TODAY readers who had won tickets for the concert, screamed and applauded from their stage-front seats, armed with pennants ($1) and posters ($2 and up).

Presley, who first broke onto the music scene in 1955, has been one of America's most consistently popular performers. He has sold millions of records and has starred in more than two dozen films. The musical *Bye Bye Birdie* was inspired by the pandemonium among teen-agers when he was drafted into the Army in 1958.

Most recently, Presley has confined his personal appearances to two yearly month-long engagements in the Las Vegas Hilton Hotel where he holds a record for show attendance, and an annual summer tour of 10 cities. He still lives in Memphis, which has just renamed a main street Elvis Presley Boulevard.

Above left: This jumpsuit is called the "Memphis Indian." Above right and below: This costume is the "Blue Phoenix."

Elvis Again World's Top Male Singer

LONDON (AP)—For the 12th time in 13 years, Elvis Presley has been named the world's top male singer in the annual New Musical Express poll.

The 35-year-old king of pop also was named world's top musical personality in 1970. Britain's Cliff Richard was runner-up in both categories.

Readers of the New Musical Express, which claims 300,000 circulation, elected the American Creedence Clearwater Revival as the top world group.

That title last went to the Beatles, who were placed second this time, although they have said they are no longer a group. The Beatles kept their title as top British group, however, and their "Let It Be" was chosen as the best album of 1970.

The title of world's most popular singer went to Diana Ross.

20 Years Later, Elvis Still a Superstar

Elvis' karate name was Tiger.

Presley Tour 'A Sellout'

LOS ANGELES — The first Elvis Presley tour of 1974 is a whirlwind 24 shows in 20 consecutive days, with all dates sold out, according to Col. Tom Parker, Presley's mentor, except for March 3rd's two shows at the Astrodome, Houston, which are a private promotion in conjunction with the Livestock Show and Rodeo. These dates are not a Presley-supervised promotion.

Tickets, as usual, are staggered from $5 to $10 for all sites. Itinerary includes; Oral Roberts University, Tulsa, March 1 and 2; Houston, 3; Civic Center, Monroe, La., 4, 7-8; Coliseum, Auburn, Ala., 5; Coliseum, Montgomery, 6; Coliseum, Charlotte, 9; Civic Center, Roanoke, 10; Coliseum, Hampton, Va., 11; Coliseum, Richmond, 12 and 18; Coliseum, Greensboro, 13; Center, Murfreesboro, Tenn., 14 and 19; Coliseum, Memphis, 16, 17 and 20.

Presley will be carrying an entourage of approximately 50 singers and musicians.

Memphis Commercial Appeal   March 17, 1974

The King Delights His Subjects

Elvis Presley performed in Memphis for the first time in 13 years yesterday, with two shows at the Mid-South Coliseum drawing full houses of fiercely partisan devotees. The King was on for more than a hour, treating Memphians to something they have been able to enjoy only via movies or televisions for a long, long time. . . .

Elvis drops in on President Richard Nixon.

Elvis at 40: Criticism that he is over the hill is defied by the fans' loyalty.

FOR ELVIS, FUN BEGINS AT 40

SHIMMERING and sparkling in his outrageous black and sky-blue sequinned costume, rings flashing, Elvis Presley belted out the songs and burlesqued his own sexy image with humor.

He wiggled his hips, shook a leg, paused while the girls went bananas, grinned and wiggled again.

This wasn't the Elvis I had expected. They told me he was 40, over the hill, sulky. A spoilt star who wanted to be alone, whose Memphis Mafia of bodyguards smashed up photographers and kept the fans away. A sex symbol who was no longer sexy. Gone to fat, they said.

You could have fooled me. I saw him in Asheville, N.C., last stop of his nation-wide summer tour, and every gal in town was praying that Elvis Presley would pick her.

Maybe he is a little huskier than he was, but he hasn't lost his elasticity. Every move of that India rubber body sent his audience into a frenzy. . . .

Elvis' shows
often revealed
his offbeat
sense of humor
and his flair
for the dramatic.

Two of Elvis' best buddies: His dog Getlo (left) and his old army pal Charlie Hodge (bottom).

ELVIS IS SANTA AGAIN
Gives away two Mark IVs

January 15, 1976

Elvis Gives Away 5 More Automobiles

Entertainer Elvis Presley took time out from skiing in Vail, Colo., yesterday to give away five more automobiles, three Cadillacs and two Continental Mark IVs.

The Rocky Mountain News said the Mark IVs were given to Denver Police Capt. Jerry Kennedy, who has handled security for a number of Presley appearances, and Dr. Gerald Starkey, Denver's police medical coordinator.

Det. Ronald Pietrafeso, who has also worked Presley concerts, received a Cadillac.

The other two Cadillacs were given to two unidentified women the newspaper said.

The two Continentals are valued at about $27,000 and Pietrafeso's Cadillac at $13,000, the News said.

Denver Police Chief Art Dill said he would allow Kennedy, Starkey and Pietrafeso to keep their cars because they were off duty when they performed services for Presley.

Presley has given away as many as 10 automobiles at a time on several previous occasions in Memphis and Hollywood.

Don Kinney shows off the new car that Elvis gave him.

Elvis rewarded a surprised Mennie Person with a new El Dorado.

Fan Finds Elvis Gem of a Guy

MOBILE, Ala. (AP)— Tommy Milham waited in line 20 hours for tickets to the Elvis Presley show, and his persistence was rewarded with a startling gift. Elvis handed him a diamond ring.

"He gave it to me as a reward for my patience," the 33-year-old Milham said Friday.

He said a jeweler appraised the ring at $2,000, and added, "I don't care if the value is $2,000 or $200,000—it is not for sale."

Memphis Press-Scimitar   April 1, 1977

Elvis Admitted to Baptist Hospital

Entertainer Elvis Presley was admitted to Baptist Hospital early today after canceling a show at the last minute in Baton Rouge, La., and flying to Memphis with complaints of intestinal flu.

Dr. George C. Nichopoulos, Presley's personal physician, said the rock and roll star was admitted to Baptist about 2:30 a.m. and is undergoing treatment.

"He has intestinal flu with gastroenteritis (inflamed stomach and intestines), and that's all I can say right now," Nichopoulos said.

About 15,000 fans including Louisiana Gov. Edwin W. Edwards and many members of the Louisiana state Legislator were gathered in the Louisiana State University Assembly Center when the announcement was made last night that Elvis was canceling the show.

Howls of protest and shouts of "rip-off" filled the large hall as the announcer told the crowd ticket money would be refunded or ticket stubs could be kept to exchange for tickets to a later Elvis concert if it could be rescheduled.

All the warm-up groups had completed their acts, and the crowd had just reseated itself after intermission in preparation of Elvis' show when the announcement was made.

In 1977, Elvis' health problems become apparent because he appears tired and overweight and he reduces the length of his concert performances.

85

King of Rock, Elvis, Dead at Age 42

Stereo Review

Elvis Has Left the Building

ELVIS PRESLEY was many different things to many different people—such was the nature of his special gifts and powers—but above all else, as three widely varying new albums suggest, he was a religious man. Indeed, this may be the only part of the Elvis myths that everyone agrees on. Both Merle Haggard's *My Farewell to Elvis* and J. D. Sumner and the Stamps' *Elvis' Favorite Gospel Songs* contain tributes to Elvis that stress his religiousness. Presley's own final album, *Elvis in Concert*, is highlighted by his reading of the gospel song "How Great Thou Art," which also appears on the Sumner album; according to Sumner, Elvis always called it "my song."

These three new releases are just the crest of the first wave of Elvis-related albums we can expect to see released in the coming year. It is pointless to ask whether they were done for money or for love, since they were obviously done for both. Fallen country stars have always inspired a rash of tribute albums— there were more than a dozen for Hank Williams—and country traditions die hard. Besides, Elvis was tastelessly and relentlessly commercialized (with his blessing) all his performing life, and there is no reason to expect anything different now. . . .

On August 16, 1977, Elvis Aron Presley died at Graceland. Fans immediately gathered in front of the Music Gates.

The Memphis Commercial Appeal   August 18, 1977

Carter Says Elvis is Symbol

WASHINGTON (UPI)—President Carter said Wednesday Elvis Presley "permanently changed the face of American popular culture" and became a worldwide symbol of his country's "vitality, rebelliousness and good humor."

The President, in a statement issued by the White House on Presley's death, said the popular singer was "unique" and is "irreplaceable."

"Elvis Presley's death deprives our country of a part of itself," Carter said. "His music and his personality, fusing the styles of white country and black rhythm and blues, permanently changed the face of American popular culture."

"His following was immense and he was a symbol to the people the world over of the vitality, rebelliousness and good humor of this country," Carter said.

Carter said Presley "burst upon the scene" more than 20 years ago "with an impact that was unprecedented and will probably never be equaled."

The official funeral procession featured 16 white limousines, though many other cars trailed behind.

Friday, August 19, 1977

From 'Floral Sea'

Wailing Elvis Fans to Receive Flowers

MEMPHIS, Tenn. (UPI)—Mourning Elvis Presley fans, barred from his private funeral, were promised a last souvenir today—a single flower each from the cemetery where the rock 'n roll superstar's body is sealed in a mausoleum.

Withered flowers plucked from a sea of 2,200 floral arrangements flanking the gray marble mausoleum were to be given to the mourners, who strained Thursday for a glimpse of the white hearse that carried Presley from Graceland, his 18-room mansion, to his final resting place at Forest Hill Cemetery.

Four miles from the midtown cemetery, only a handful of the 75,000 fans who had jammed the streets of Elvis Presley Boulevard during the three-day vigil, remained in front of the white-columned, hilltop mansion where Presley died Tuesday of heart failure at the age of 42.

The official pallbearers included Joe Esposito, Dr. George Nichopoulos, Billy Smith, and Lamar Fike.

Elvis fans hang onto $600,000 worth of tickets

Had Elvis Presley lived, more than 120,000 people would have paid about $1,300,000 to hear the overweight superstar belt out his famous songs during a 12-city tour that was to have ended Sunday night in Memphis.

But when the 42-year-old Presley died of a heart attack on Aug. 16, one day before the tour was to have begun, he left more than a legacy behind him.

Promoters, theater owners, and lawyers must now tackle a problem they rarely encounter—what to do with an estimated $600,000 in tickets adoring fans refuse to give up. . . .

Fans held onto their tickets for the tour that never was.

Vernon gave the funeral flowers to the legions of fans who mourned at the gates of Graceland.

This Inscription on Elvis' Tomb

*He was a precious gift from God
We cherished and loved dearly.*

*He had a God-given talent that he shared
With the world. And without a doubt,
He became most widely acclaimed;
Capturing the hearts of young and old alike.*

*He was admired not only as an entertainer,
But as the great humanitarian that he was;
For his generosity, and his kind feeling
For his fellow man.*

*He revolutionized the field of music and
Received its highest awards.*

*He became a living legend in his own time,
Earning the respect and love of millions.*

*God saw that he needed some rest and
Called him home to be with Him.*

*We miss you, Son and Daddy. I thank God
That He gave us you as our son.*

By Vernon Presley

Vernon Presley paid tribute to his son in this poignant inscription at his gravesite.

" He never really died and never will.... He cut a path through the world! He's gonna be history, man. "

-Carl Perkins

PHOTO CREDITS:

Front cover: **Cinema Collectors:** (top left, top right & bottom center); **Sharon Fox Collection:** (bottom left); **Photofest:** (bottom right); **Ger Rijff Collection:** (right center).

AP/Wide World Photos: 18 (top right), 30 (bottom), 31 (top), 40 (top), 42, 43 (bottom), 56 (top), 70, 74 (top), 84 (top), 87 (top), 88, 90; **Dolores Balcom Collection:** 61 (bottom); **Corbis-Bettmann:** 76 (right); Corbis: 11 (bottom left & bottom right), 15 (bottom), 16 (bottom), 19 (top), 40 (bottom), 67 (top), 86 (top), 87 (bottom); **Cinema Collectors:** end sheet, contents (right), 33 (bottom), 34 (bottom right), 35, 47 (top), 50 (bottom), 51 (top), 54 (top & center), 55 (left center), 59 (bottom), 60 (right), 62 (top), 64 (bottom left & bottom right), 69; **Bill DeNight Collection:** 89 (top); **Susan Doll Collection:** 17 (bottom); **Sharon Fox Collection:** 9 (bottom), 10, 13 (top), 14, 15 (top), 17 (top), 24, 25, 26 (bottom), 27 (bottom left), 43 (top), 44 (bottom), 45 (top & bottom), 46 (bottom), 48 (top), 51 (left center & right center), 54 (bottom), 56 (left center, right center & bottom), 57 (top & center), 63 (top left & top right), 65, 68 (top left), 71 (top right & bottom left), 73, 74 (bottom), 76 (left), 78 (left), 80 (top), 81 (left); Elvis Presley Enterprises, Inc.: 71 (bottom right); United Press International: 21 (top), 29 (top), 41 (top), 59 (top), 84 (bottom); **The Kobal Collection:** 64 (top); **Motion Picture & Television Photo Archive:** 44 (top), 47 (bottom), 49 (top), 58, 71 (top left), 72 (top); Bert Mittleman: 12 (top); Gabi Rona: 22 (bottom left & bottom right); Bob Willoughby: 38 (bottom); **Photofest:** 6 (bottom); **Photoplay Archives/LGI Photo Agency:** 13 (bottom left), 19 (bottom), 20 (bottom left), 21 (bottom), 22 (top left), 24 (top left & top right), 27 (bottom right), 30 (top), 32, 33 (top), 36 (bottom); **Ger Rijff Collection:** contents (bottom), 6 (center), 18 (top left), 20 (bottom right), 26 (top), 34 (bottom left), 36 (top), 38 (top), 55 (top), 61 (top); BM Studios: 8 (bottom); **Robin C. Rosaaen Collection:** 6 (top), 7, 8 (top), 9 (top left), 11 (top), 12 (bottom), 13 (bottom right), 16 (top), 20 (top), 28, 29 (bottom), 34 (top), 37, 45 (center), 46 (top), 48 (bottom), 49 (bottom), 50 (top), 52 (top & center), 53, 57 (bottom), 60 (left), 62 (bottom left & bottom right), 66, 67 (bottom), 68 (bottom left), 72 (bottom), 75, 78 (right & bottom), 79 (left), 80 (bottom), 81 (right), 82, 83, 86 (bottom), 89 (bottom), 91; Keith Alverson: 79 (right & bottom), 85 (top); Maria Luisa Davies: 68 (top right & bottom right); Elvis Presley Museum: 9 (top right), 23, 27 (top), 31 (bottom), 39 (top), 52 (bottom); HEIS: 85 (bottom); George O. Hill, II: 81 (bottom); R. Leech: 77; Memories of Elvis, Inc.: 7.

Additional Photography: Sam Griffith Photography; Brian Warling Photography; Dave Szarzak/White Eagle Studios.
Photo Tinting Artist: Cheryl Winser.

Additional Copyright Information:

Dig, ©1957, p.24; ©1956 Elvis Presley Enterprises, pp. 18, 25; "Kentucky Rain" sheet music, ©1968, p.65; Elvis' recordings, ©1956, 1960, 1961, 1963, 1969, 1972, 1973, RCA, pp. 10, 11, 45, 51, 54, 65, 73, 76; ©Sun Records, 1956, p. 6; *TV Guide* ©1960 Triangle Publication, p. 44.